# ODYSSEY:
## LOVE *and* TERROR
### *in* GREECE, 1969

## STEVE FOX

To Emily!
may Odysseys teach &
heal you!
Best,
Steve

For information, contact Nighthawk Press:
www.nighthawkpress.com

ISBN: 978-0615973852
Library of Congress Control Number: 2014933703

Cover photograph © Steve Fox
Cover design by Kathleen Munroe, Starr Design, Littleton, Colorado,
    www.starrdesign.biz
Interior design and copyediting: Barbara Scott, Final Eyes, Taos,
    New Mexico, www.finaleyes.net
Editing: Bonnie Lee Black, Taos, New Mexico, www.bonnieleeblack.com
Author photograph by Kathleen Brennan

For a listing of interior photography, see last page

NIGHTHAWK PRESS
TAOS, NEW MEXICO
www.nighthawkpress.com

*for Allan Wenger,*

*Linda Carter,*

*and Donna LeFurgey*

# ONE

*If the cops see me I'm dead. This car has no speed. When I make it out of these narrow, twisty streets, I'll have to cross the edge of downtown. There'll be more cops on the wider roads, and it'll be easier to see me. How can I outrun anyone in this 44-horsepower VW bug, especially against their souped-up Fiats and Mercedes? They know Athens way better than I do. They're better drivers, too. I've already had one accident here in this thing. Driving in Greece is high risk.*

I was on a secret mission for my American friends Allan and Linda Wenger in June 1969. Allan was one of the coolest guys I'd ever met, someone I'd do nearly anything for. He was about 30, six years older than I, a bit shorter than my five feet eleven, with long black sideburns, receding hair, a resonant baritone voice and hipster ankle boots. Linda was also 30 or thereabouts, a petite blond with long, luxurious hair, china-blue eyes and a heartbreaker smile. I didn't know when or whether I'd ever see them again. They had just fled Greece because of their involvement in a group resisting the country's military dictators.

These dictators, known to everyone in Greece as "the Colonels," a far-right military junta that had been in power for three years, fully embraced the eastern Mediterranean tradition of torturing their critics. Their preferred method was called *falanga*, from the Greek word meaning the clusters of finger or toe bones arrayed together. Torturers beat the bottom of the feet with iron pipes, which leaves no marks, but is particularly brutal and painful because it damages the clusters of nerve endings, small bones and tendons in the feet and cripples your ability to run, or even walk well, for months.

I was a new lieutenant serving in the U.S. Air Force at the Athenai Air Base, which was half of Athens International Airport. Allan and Linda had become like a big brother and sister to me. In the six months I'd known them, Allan and Linda had never told me they were in a resistance group because of the danger my U.S. military affiliation could bring to their 25 comrades, who were already risking their health and lives by defying the Colonels. But they were forced to tell me about their involvement when Allan was pulled over by cops while driving the couple's red VW bug a week before. He went on the torture list and left on the next plane for Paris to keep the police from getting to Linda and the rest of the resistance group through him. Linda and Allan knew he was the lightning rod who could endanger all of them if he didn't vanish immediately.

I had helped Linda pack up their stuff. A week after Allan left, she and their newborn baby girl, Niki, got on the same early flight Allan had. Then I was alone in Athens with the knowledge that the cops had probably photographed my car, a primer-gray '66 VW decorated with three saucer-sized flower decals. They were symbols from the Summer of Love in the U.S. two years before. Now, knowing how far-right the Colonels were, I found myself wishing I had removed them. Linda told me that Allan said the cops surely must have photographed my car in the last two weeks while they were surveilling Allan. I had parked in front of their house on Dafnomili Street on the slopes of Lykabettos Hill many times over the past five months.

*Is this the intersection where I bear right? Too late, I've done it. Then right at the next light? Deep breaths. Stay cool. Don't worry — oh, Jesus, check the gas gauge! Half a tank, thank God. Would've been brilliant to run out of gas. Wish I knew who's gonna meet me when I get to the drop spot.*

I glanced warily at the two-by-two-foot cardboard box on the passenger seat beside me. The mission with this box makes me an enemy of the Greek dictators, although inside the box was only a mimeograph machine. Just like the hand-crank ones we had in grade school in the fifties, with their aromatic purple ink. To the Colonels, this humble machine was more dangerous than a bomb, because it told the truth and it exposed their evil lies.

Allan and Linda had been making English translations of their group's fliers, which the other members then spread around the streets of Athens. These pamphlets were the only independent source of news in this European capital city. They exposed the truth about who was in custody or being tortured, who had escaped the country, and what the "wonderful tranquility" the Colonels were bringing to Greece really meant. The Colonels had arrested 10,000 people the first day of their coup in 1967, throwing them in various prisons on the islands dotting the Aegean. They had closed down all radio, print and TV news, and banned meetings with more than five people attending. The mimeograph was the social-media delivery system of the day. The Colonels were using an identical hand-crank machine to print their own propaganda.

*Okay, stop. Look both ways. Ahead and behind, too. It'll be treason if they catch me. With Allan and Linda gone, there's nobody to help me if I get caught. I don't know anyone else in their group, they don't know me, and they wouldn't risk helping an American officer. Would my Air Force bosses help me? Ha! I'd be a traitor to them, too. Do I have the status and rights of an Air Force officer, an American citizen, a brother? Or am I an enemy to both sides? Good friggin' questions. Dusk coming on now. Streetlights flickering. Put your lights on! Check the rearview. Don't panic and run a light or a stop sign. I should have taken the flower decals off when they shipped the car over from Mississippi. Too late to tell myself not to panic.*

The mimeograph machine was just one of the thousand things the Colonels had explicitly banned from private possession. All Western literature and music were on their massive list. From mini-skirts and the Beatles to Socrates and Plato. And if they caught you with anything on the list, you were out of luck, because there were no more civilian courts, no lawyers, no judges. Just the Colonels.

*Crossroads — which way? Can't sit here wondering. Where's the map? Okay, left here, not right. Is that guy following me? Fuck! No, he turned off. Just one more turn and I should be at the drop point.*

"Destroy this map as soon as you see where it leads you. Park at this spot," Linda had hurriedly pointed out on the map, "and blink your lights once. Don't look at or speak to whoever opens your car door to take the box, OK? Don't look at them or say anything! And good luck." She looked so stressed. "Steve, Allan wanted you to know he loves you like a brother. And I do too. We're both in your debt for helping us get out of here. I'm so sorry we'll be gone by the time you deliver the box." She seemed worried. Niki was crying. Linda had been having irregular heartbeat. I was worried for her.

I only had two friends left in Athens now — a self-involved name-dropping deejay at the American base radio station and my American girlfriend, Deborah Cuomo, back at my house in Glyfada, waiting for me. Her father was a chief master sergeant, who managed the day-to-day activities of Iraklion Air Base on Crete, the main U.S. spy base in the eastern Mediterranean. I knew that, because of her father, Deborah had to be really careful not to get caught up in this resistance activity.

When I arrived in Greece in 1968, Allan and Linda had already been in Athens for four years. They knew writers, film people, the nightlife scenes — and they were fun to be with. They were from New York, where Allan had been a folk singer in the Greenwich Village folk revival of the sixties. Allan was my mentor, my idol. He and I had already dubbed a "Spaghetti Western" film into English. It was being dubbed into Spanish and French, too, under Greek direction. We had acted together in the Edward Albee two-man play *Zoo Story,* which Allan also directed.

*Oh! My traffic accident two months ago! The cop took my ID info and license number! Was that cop in the same division as the ones who were photographing Allan's visitors? Would traffic cops match accident reports to the Security Police's enemies lists? OK, the map says last right turn here. Really dark now. We're close, Mimeo! Who would have guessed that a humble VW bug could execute a spy mission or that an innocent ditto machine like the ones we all knew from church and school could be a tool of revolution?*

The drop point was on a straight uphill street. I stopped about a hundred yards past the last house and cut the engine.

*Blink the lights once. Just wait.*

I was concentrating so hard I could hear my watch ticking and crickets outside in the weeds. Nothing happened. A minute. *Should I blink the lights again? No, Linda's note said <u>once</u>.* A car started up. I hadn't noticed it parked off the street as I passed. It slowly drove up behind me. I didn't look at it, even in my mirror. My heart pounded in my chest and in my ears. *Please please let it not be the cops.* My passenger door opened. It took all I had not to look over.

The hair stood out on my arms, and the goosebumps surged up my nape. I stared straight ahead. *What if they'd already infiltrated Allan's group?* The box scraped across the seat cover. The door closed quietly and clicked. The car behind me backed up, turned a 180 and sped away. I looked at the empty seat beside me and got chills again. I drove off nonchalantly for several blocks before I remembered my lights. *Shit! Turn them back on!*

*Now zig-zag back to downtown. Punch in the cigarette lighter. Pull over by this warehouse. Get the corner of the map into the glow of the lighter. Let the flame grow. Toss the map out of the window. Watch it curl in flames and burn to ash. Drive home by a roundabout route.*

# TWO

In late January 1967, two years before I drove that mimeograph machine across Athens, my second semester of grad school at the University of Texas in Austin was just getting underway. My part-time job was news reporting, afternoons and weekends, at station KTBC AM-FM TV, owned by Lyndon and Lady Bird Johnson, at that time the president and first lady. It was the biggest, most well-connected media station in Austin, the state capital, and I felt lucky to be working there. It was the doorway to a career for me, if that's what I wanted.

In addition to my news-reading shifts, I had started hosting an afternoon music show. One day, I politely asked the station general manager whether, in addition to the Dean Martin, Frank Sinatra, Rosie Clooney and Brothers Four songs that seemed to dominate our music library, I could play some Bob Dylan. He refused with a sneer. "Steve, we do not play rock and roll at this station."

"But Dylan's a poet more than a rocker. His whole start has been based on Woody Guthrie folk songs. I don't want to play his latest songs. I know the weirder stuff on his recent albums is not right for our audience. I just want to play one song for you to consider: it's called 'Love Minus Zero, No Limit.'"

I thought that was a safe song to introduce Dylan to this radio station. It had vivid images, but none of Dylan's ridiculing tone and surreal images, like his albums *Highway 61 Revisited* and *Blonde on Blonde*. I thought anybody listening would see it was more like a country love song. It ended with "My love, she's like a raven/at my window with a broken wing."

The general manager stared at me from his deep baggy eyes and answered, "Lady Bird Johnson has an office on the top floor, son, and she might be in the halls at any time. Do you understand?"

One day, half an hour before my music show, I found a note on the control room door: "Steve — registered mail for you in the newsroom."

I walked over to the newsroom, and a colleague handed me the registered letter and a receipt to sign. It was from Selective Service. In effect, it was a note from Lyndon Johnson, who was calling for more troops to fight the Vietnam War.

"We said you weren't a flight risk," said Phil, my news colleague. "The mail guy let us sign for it." The other guys sidled around.

"Uh-oh," said one. "What does Uncle Sam want now?" I ripped it open and read out loud: "Greetings, you have been chosen for induction into the Armed Forces of the U.S." A chorus arose from my newsroom colleagues, all huddled around me with their ties loosened three or four inches and their collars open.

"Sam wants you, man."

"No way, Steve."

"But you're in grad school. How can they draft you?"

I read on: "You are ordered to report to the nearest induction center for your physical examination. If you pass the exam, you are to enlist immediately in the branch of U.S. military service of your choice, or accept assignment to the U.S. Army by June 30."

"We need you over there reporting the dirty news, not carrying a rifle," one of the guys said in a low tone.

All the air seemed to have gone out of my lungs. I stared straight ahead at nothing as I remembered the boring English course I had dropped two weeks before, after the first class meeting. Could the university have already reported me as "not full time?"

"So any of you know what my options are for this?" I asked.

A pause. Of course they didn't know about — or couldn't risk discussing in that room — alternatives to the draft in the midst of the Vietnam buildup. Hey, the newsroom was bugged, for all we knew.

"I need to take a walk, guys. Can someone cover my air times?"

One of them told me to take the whole shift off, that he'd cover for me. I headed out the newsroom door and down the hall, questions swirling in my brain. *Would I have to leave grad school* and *this job? I was never supposed to get drafted.*

It had been exciting to join this newsroom four months earlier. It crackled with electricity. The day I started, August 15th, they were still reporting on the nation's first maniac to be called a mass murderer, Charles Whitman. On August first, he had put the cross hairs of his rifle scope on people as they walked 280 feet below his sniper perch on the Texas Tower, the centerpiece of this huge campus. His murder rampage provoked a hail of return fire when the news went out over the radio that a sniper, or several of them, was atop the tower. My boss, the news director, was the only reporter in a mobile unit who got within range of Whitman's bullets to report live on the shootings as they were happening and feed reports to all three networks.

My colleagues found out later, as they conducted hundreds of interviews, that much of the return fire at Whitman came from ordinary guys and ex-military dudes who rushed home, or to their pickups, to get their deer rifles and surplus Army carbines. One guy walked into a store, bought a box of ammo and a six-pack, and headed out to find a good spot to sip a brew and squeeze off a few rounds at whoever was up there. The Austin police, like most cities, did not yet have a SWAT team.

Adrenaline had surged through Austin's weekend marksmen, some of whom took up positions on the roofs of neighboring university buildings and winged bullets through the drain holes in the parapet surrounding the observation deck where Whitman was concealed. Puffs of atomized Texas sandstone appeared, as .270, .30-30, .300 Savage and various other .30-caliber bullets pocked the top levels of the main symbol of the university. Two guys in a Cessna took off with a deer rifle and buzzed the tower. They didn't get off a shot, but they were able to radio the airport, which relayed to the police below that there was only one man up there, not a whole gang, as people feared.

Finally, Whitman was killed by an off-duty cop who climbed the 27 floors with an off-duty security officer. They made their way past the body of the woman who admitted people to the observation deck of the tower and up the last flight of sticky, bloody stairs and the bodies of two tourists who'd picked the wrong day to visit the tower. But since Whitman had ripped the only phone off its wire when he killed the attendant, the two officers had no way to get word down to the forces encircling the tower that Whitman was dead. So bullets from cops, deputies, security guards and Austin's deer-hunting militia continued to pin the heroes down for another half hour. Whitman had killed 16 and wounded 20 more. A reporter coined the term "mass murderer" for Whitman, and it stuck as a fearful category of crime ever since.

When I arrived in Austin a week later, the office of my grad advisor in English, on the 17th floor of the tower, was still draped with police tape, while my TV news job also sent me to the tower for photos of bullet holes. We were still doing follow-up stories four months later when my draft notice came. Whitman's sickening outburst added to the macabre stories we read to our radio listeners every half hour about the growing lists of wounded and killed in Vietnam, and to the equally well-covered violence against the civil rights movement in Mississippi and Alabama.

The shocks of the sixties had begun for me and for the entire nation when John Fitzgerald Kennedy was assassinated in Dallas in 1963, three years before the UT–Austin tower incident. JFK's killing as he rode through admiring throngs with his lovely young wife, Jackie, in her pink suit and pillbox hat, was an unspeakably tragic end to their reign over our hearts.

The press had begun calling the Kennedy presidency "Camelot," after the Broadway play, which depicted an idyllic vision of the English King Arthur, played by Richard Burton, his radiant queen Guinevere, played by Julie Andrews, and their knight Lancelot, played by Robert Goulet. King Arthur tells a youth at the play's end:

> Don't let it be forgot
> That once there was a spot,
> For one brief, shining moment
> That was known as Camelot.

The play was the Kennedy couple's favorite, with its signature song predicting "happy-ever-aftering" for the greatest English king of legend and his beautiful wife. The play opened in 1960 and ran until January 1963, and was in the first year of a two-year national tour when JFK was killed. They had to cancel the tour when the head of the Round Table was murdered. At his inauguration in 1961, Kennedy was only 43 and Jackie only 31. They were sleek, athletic, charismatic, flirty, and rich, with two adorable kids, Carolyn and John

Jr. They personified the handsome young family, the New Frontier, the new generation that would send men to the moon; my college friends and I were dazzled by their charisma, even though my own hometown, Dallas, was a hotbed for Kennedy hate and outrage over his stand on civil rights for African Americans.

So when JFK died and Jackie's shocked, mourning face looked out through a black veil at the state funeral for her husband, with tiny young John saluting his father's casket as it passed a few yards in front of him, the entire country fell into a deeply shared national bereavement. For me, my parents had divorced a year before that, and I had become estranged from them, especially my dad, not only from the bitterness of their divorce but also because they disapproved of Kennedy and opposed new civil rights laws. I hadn't wrapped my head around the grief of my own family's disintegration when the nation's Camelot family was blown apart on the same stretch of road that I had ridden on to Sunday School week in and week out.

I opened the production department door. "Stephen!" Pickle said, beaming. My friends Pickle and Tim and Niz, good ol' Texas boys, were the film crew for the station. Gary was the son of our local Congressman, J.J. "Jake" Pickle, and Tim had been accepted to the Naval Academy at Annapolis. He had decided to quit after his first semester there. He, Gary, and Niz had welcomed me, in my Buddy Holly glasses, into their Three Musketeers lives. They were in the film "bidness" and were devoted to drinkin' and fun. They had memorized all of Marlon Brando's lines in "One-Eyed Jacks" and recited them at the parties they threw for their weekend film company.

"It's Steve the newsman! Or is it the deejay?" said Tim. I showed them my draft letter. Pickle was straight with me: "Damn, Steve, there must be somebody who could help you get outta this, but I don't know 'em. I can't, with my dad and all, you know that." His dad had been in Congress for several terms and, we knew from his son's stories, had felt LBJ's breath on his face and claw on his shoulder more than once.

Tim said, "Don't go, man. You're no more cut out for it than I was." But neither of them had been drafted. They both somberly repeated that they didn't know who around campus or the bar scene or coffeehouse circuit might know somebody who knew somebody who handled these things. "I guess people go to Canada," Niz said. "Don't know if you can come back, though," he said with a sheepish grin.

I thanked them. These guys were like the brothers I never had. Maybe they were also filling in for the father I'd lost in my parents' divorce. But it was my decision to make. I walked out into the sunlight of downtown Austin through the state capitol grounds, acres of well-kept lawn and dark live-oak trees with branches spreading to the ground.

That night, eating my hamburger and hash browns in a corner booth at a local diner, I turned this abrupt change of events over in my mind. *It feels so good to be away from home. Maybe being further away would feel even better.* After my dad and older sister moved out of our house in Dallas, I was left at 16 with my mom and her grief. We lost the house, and I had to help her find an apartment and buy a car. In her fury, Mom convinced me that she was the wronged party. The lawyers agreed that I couldn't see my dad until 90 days had passed. It became all mom, all the time.

As we struggled to deal with our isolation and drop in income, she said to me on a number of occasions, "A boy becomes a man when a man's needed." She said I was the man of the house now. I didn't want to take my dad's place. Her favorite quote about her situation

was a line from Macbeth: "Hell hath no fury like a woman scorned."
I had to listen to her crying jags. She lost about 20 pounds in three
months. Once she sagged against me, crying, her face a grimace, and I
felt overwhelmed by her grief.

One day before I moved to Austin, she started crying again
and said, "Oh God, son, I haven't just mothered you, I've *smothered*
you. I thought I'd maybe cut off the sashes of one of my aprons and
put them in a box and give them to you." I felt torn between numb-
ness to all my parents' problems and my need to get far, far away.

I sacrificed many weekends at North Texas State University to
hitchhike home to keep my mom company, buck up her spirits and
help her with "man of the house" things. I felt for her deeply, not only
because she had just lost her husband, my dad, but also because I was
so indebted to her. She was the one who taught me to love language.
She gave me the foundation for grad school and the radio-station job
through her love of puns and dialect sayings from French, German
and Spanish: *"Besa me mucho." "Honni soit qui mal y pense." "Sitzen sie,
das ist alles."* And one from Pennsylvania Dutch: "Trow da horse over
da fence some more hay." I had been a language student of hers from
my toddler days.

But it was time for me to go. I knew I'd get out of the cage of her
grief eventually. It didn't occur to me then that maybe by being the
Good Son, I was avoiding the risks of freedom. Was I hiding for my
own sake as much as helping her? Either way, I needed to get out.

At the diner, I got a refill on my coffee and made a list:

   – *Austin's the hippest town in Texas*
   – *But the military offers the world*
   – *A job at LBJ's station is a plum*
   – *But Dean Martin, not Bob Dylan*
   – *Lady Bird in the hallway*

*Could my idols Joan Didion or Norman Mailer stand working in Lyndon's newsroom? All I do is rip and read stories from the AP newswire.*

I looked out the plate-glass windows at the rush-hour traffic, shifting my focus from the street to my own reflection, looking at myself looking at the traffic. How, it occurred to me with a tingling in my stomach, could I not have noticed how much I wanted to get out of Texas?

The next day, with a January wind whipping the bare trees, I headed to the TV station to give them my notice. I couldn't put into words what I felt. My desires to follow this challenge out of Texas and into the world coalesced so quickly that I never looked for the underground draft-resister network. I'd never heard of it, anyway. Never sat down with a Tarot reader or looked for a wise man. Didn't know where you found such people. I never met a veteran: nobody in my family had ever been in the military, going back three generations on both my parents' sides.

I chose enlisting over running. It was visceral and below the level of my understanding: I was hungry for experience. *Something's calling me. I'm game.*

# THREE

I stood, holding my thumb high, on the shoulder of Interstate 57 halfway between Chicago and Champaign, Illinois. I had taken a flight from Dallas to Chicago and was hitchhiking south to Champaign. Faded jeans, of course, Clark's desert boots, black leather jacket from a thrift store. My hair was just over the tops of my ears and down my forehead. I was out on the prairie, shivering in the frigid March wind.

I was on my way to visit my best friend from college, my old roommate, Jim Cuomo, one of the jazzers who'd been drawn to my North Texas State school in Denton for its BFA degree programs in jazz playing and music composition, the only ones in the country. The guys who came for those programs were an insurgency of hipsters in Denton. Now, newly drafted, I was drawn to visit Jim and his cool buddies before I had to report for Army induction. I had signed up for the Army Signal Corps officer program because it was a two-year commitment and all the other military branches required four years.

The cars and trucks whizzed by me at 70 miles per hour, blasting my hair back with their wind. I watched each sun-reflecting, bugsplotched windshield zoom toward me: big fifties Buicks with vertical grill bars like metal baleen whales. Ford and Chevy pickups with farm gear and hay bales in back. VW buses with hippies at the wheel. And every once in a while an MG-TD or an Austin-Healey, the driver wearing aviator shades. I was overcome with the fantasy of joining such a dude on a sophisticated voyage, flipping toggle switches on the walnut dash and exchanging our vast library of knowledge about legendary drivers like Stirling Moss or Juan Fangio. I'd read about them in *Sports Illustrated.*

Here between Chicago and Champaign, the river of Americans zooming by me was like a Fourth of July parade — goofy, playful, friendly, hard-knuckled, deviant. I was fascinated.

A white Chrysler hardtop pulled over. A big, handsome guy was driving and a woman was lounging beside him. I settled into the back.

"Where you headed?" the driver asked. I told him Champaign.

"You a student at U of I?" he asked over his shoulder.

"No. Visiting a friend. My old college roommate from North Texas State. Sort of a last hurrah. I'm going into the service." The man swiveled his rear-view mirror to see me in the back seat.

"What branch?" he asked.

"Army. Got drafted. Signed up with the Signal Corps. Headed for Europe. Or maybe Seattle."

"So you have an assignment over there?"

"No," I said, "I haven't had basic yet."

The leaves of seven-feet-tall dried corn plants standing in rows in the fields gestured in the breeze like arms. After a minute he said, "Buddy, do you actually think the Army intends to send you where you want to go?"

"Well, they asked me to list three places I wanted to be posted. Said it was a contract they'd honor."

"Jesus Christ!" the driver growled. He gripped the steering wheel with one big mitt. His wife or girlfriend or whatever she was glanced at him.

"Look," he said to me into the rear-view mirror. "I'm an Air Force recruiting coordinator. Not just a recruiter — a *coordinator* for the region. Do you realize that the Pentagon is *doubling* the number of troops in Vietnam, as we speak? You think they're going to say, 'Let's put this guy in London or Paris or wherever he'll be happy'?"

Jazz was playing softly on the radio. They were so at ease, tooling along at 55. It was surreal that he represented the military. My dad had pleaded with me not to go near Vietnam, and I thought this contract with the Signal Corps accomplished that.

"Well," I said. "He said it was a legal contract."

"Sure he did. Did you read the fine print? Believe me, buddy, this is my business. You have exactly *zero* chance of going to London or Paris or the Pacific Northwest. They're in the body business, not the 'where would you like to live' business. All decisions about where you serve belong to them. Why do you think you got drafted? You and thousands more? They didn't ask you if you wanted to go, did they?"

He was staring right through me in the mirror. Now we were passing gas stations and warehouses and restaurants as we entered Champaign. Finally we introduced ourselves.

"I'm Leland Rucker, Steve. Senior master sergeant in recruiting," he said. "Here's the truth. For a college grad like you, the Air Force would be more like working for a corporation than being in a war. I can have you switched to the Air Force, accepted into Officer Training School, and you can avoid getting your butt shot off and watching body bags fill up with your buddies in 'Nam. Get yourself to the nearest induction center — from here, it's Indianapolis — give them this card within 24 hours, and I guarantee they'll switch you. I'll call and tell them as soon as I let you off in Champaign."

He held the card out over his shoulder, and I took it. I liked this guy. I believed him more than the Army recruiter who had his enlistment quotas for that week and month posted right on the wall. He steered the Chrysler to the curb in front of my old roommate's house.

"Think hard about it, Steve. Could change your life."

The twin pipes of their cruiser resonated as they pulled away.

I stood by the curb under a line of huge elm trees and felt waves of excitement criss-crossing in my stomach. I watched the big car until it disappeared. My road had just forked and I was stunned. Was that guy an angel? Like the TV show "The Millionaire," he didn't know me but he had just given me a huge gift.

I walked up the steps of the big two-story frame house and knocked. Big-band jazz and a pungent odor wafted out of the screen door. I couldn't see anybody. I cupped my hands around my eyes and pressed my forehead into the screen. "Jim?" I said.

A female voice, flat and ironic, said, "I'm down here."

I swiveled my gaze down. I saw huge brown eyes and wide cheekbones.

"Sorry, I didn't see you," I said.

"It's OK. You must be the famous roommate from Texas," she said with a half-smile as she opened the door. I stepped in. Dusk was coming on. I heaved my pack inside and stuck out my hand.

"I'm Steve. Who are you?"

"I'm Deborah. The sister from college in San Antonio." I glanced at her curves. Her miniskirt barely covered her. Her face said 14 but her voice and attitude said college. Her body said woman.

She grinned, her eyes gleaming. "Nothin' like a little cognitive dissonance, huh?"

Wow! She was droll, she was sexy. I was fascinated. As my eyes adjusted, I saw guys sprawled around a sofa and some overstuffed chairs farther into the room. An announcer was shouting "Dizzy Gillespie! Dizzy Gillespie!" over the applause and whistling. The sofa and chairs were docked at a big coffee table covered with ashtrays, record albums and sheet music.

"Steve-o!" Deborah's brother, Jim, walked toward me, beaming, wearing loose pleated pants, a buttoned short-sleeve shirt that hung down to his butt, a Fu Manchu mustache, and a fedora. He was holding a short cigarette between his thumb and first finger. He was nearly a head taller than Deborah, and he was only five-four.

"Jimmy! You look like the fourth Marx Brother," I said, as we hugged.

He laughed. "The *fifth* Marx brother!" he said. "Don't forget Zeppo. So you've met my sister, and these are the guys in the university jazz band. Say hello to the *yazz bando*. Guys, meet my prodigal roommate."

"Hey, man," said the jazzers, as I held out my hand. No crunching grips like in Texas — mostly fingertip touches. A big angular guy, slicked back blond hair down to his collar, looking like a 35-year-old ex-con, made room for me on the couch and said, "Welcome to Shampoo-Ipana." The guy on the other side of me offered a short stub of a joint. I was among the minuscule percentage of college grads in 1967 who had never been around marijuana, even though I knew lots of drama majors and jazzers. *Time to check it out,* I thought. The guy patiently held his index finger against my thumb as I tried to grasp the short joint. When I sucked at it, the glowing ember tumbled down my shirt and began to burn a hole. I stood up and brushed at it, giving the joint back to the guy to relight.

"Where can I get some water?" I asked.

Deborah said, "Hey, come out to the kitchen. We'll clean that up, and we've got some snacks. You must be hungry after hitching in that wind."

The kitchen was a maze of musical instrument cases, bottles and fast-food trash. Deborah cleared us a place at a white enamel table. She was a montage of contrasts. The way she navigated through the crowd of musicians … her *attitude* … a slouch, a bold looseness. Not like a shy little sister at all. She looked directly at me with a broad smile. Her long lashes and dark eyebrows arched above her eyes and a smile fold framed them below. I looked back into those eyes with my own smile, which I had no control over. She seemed just cracked-up about the whole scene. I wondered what Jim had told her about me.

"So D.H. Lawrence, is it? That's what Jimmy tells me you've been studying? The Chatterleys, and other sexy couples?"

"Yep. Grad seminar. I wasn't too into it until the prof said they had three versions of *Lady Chatterley* in the tower archives. Lawrence's typescripts that I could study to write a term paper on. Even had D.H.'s notes on some pages. So I did."

"No shit?" She leaned back in her chair. "That's the one I read. D.H. actually got the words penis and vulva published, and that was in 1921. *Vulva!*" she giggled. "Sounds like somebody's dog in Yugoslavia. 'Here, Vulva!'" We both blurted laughter. "We all passed it around at Our Lady of the Lake."

The jazz in the other room, the mess in this kitchen, the buzz I felt talking about D.H. Lawrence with this grinning elf who'd actually read him: This is good, I thought. This is fun.

"I read *Women in Love,* too," said Deborah, putting a bag of chips and a bowl of peanuts on the table. She said that Lawrence's books and everything else interesting were blacklisted at Lady of the Lake, but they were in the city library.

"So Lady of the Lake is a college?" I asked.

"Yup," she said, raking the burger wrappers and cold fries and empty ketchup packets into a trash bag. She got up and walked a few steps to the fridge, came back with two Cokes, set them down in the clearing between us, and sat cross-legged in her chair, gaining a few inches of altitude. She reached up her side and pulled down on the elastic of her bra: a soft snap. "Finished my first year there, and that's enough. Heading off to Crete with the parents. Help me, Jesus!" She burst into a rolling cackle and covered her mouth with one hand. Her breasts jiggled as she laughed. She noticed that I noticed, which made her laugh more. Some Coke shot into her nose and we both cracked up at her coughing attack. She had to wipe her eyes with a napkin from the pile. She tried to calm down. There were teardrops on her long lashes. "Oh Lord," she said, blowing her nose on a napkin. *God, she's fun!* I thought. *Jim never told me about her!*

I asked why she was going with her parents to Crete. She said their dad was a career Air Force guy, and she'd have free housing and food, cheap stuff at the BX — the base store — and free flights to mainland Greece and other parts of Europe. She had a little sister about eleven and a brother six, so they'd keep Mom busy and Deborah could bop all over the Mediterranean.

"Father in the Air Force? I didn't know that. I was just picked up in the middle of nowhere by an Air Force guy! I'm going into the Air Force myself," I said.

"Oh yeah? Jimmy told me you were going into the Army. You didn't sound like the type. And you don't look the type. Are you really going into the Air Force now?"

"Yeah. I am. I met this recruiter guy just now who gave me a ride into Champaign. He switched me from the Army to the Air Force. Gotta go over to Indianapolis tomorrow and finalize it."

"Well, hey," she said. "That's bold! Maybe you can get a flight to Crete and we can go find ol' King Minos and go through the maze."

Now we're talkin'. "Yeah! That would be fun!" I said. Jim and two of his buddies came scuffing into the kitchen.

"Aha! Here they are, stoned again!" Jim crowed, leering at us. "Thanks for feeding him, Debbie."

*Are we stoned?* I thought. *But I didn't smoke.*

Deborah looked at me. "Call me Deb or Deborah, but never Debbie," she said. A couple more guys came into the kitchen and it appeared that the jazzers had a softball game scheduled. My crush-inducing interlude with Deb was over. She looked at me, smiling broadly, and said, "See yez later," using the Chicago second-person plural, and walked out.

"Hey, don't feel you gotta be nice to my sister," Jim said. "She's just escaped Our Lady of the Snake, or somethin' like that, down in San Antonio."

"No," I said, "she's really smart. I like her."

Jim looked at me with disbelief. "You what? You do? She's really a motormouth, man."

"I know! And a damn good one! How could she not be, with you as her brother?"

That night, several guys crashed on the floor, along with me and Deb. I lay awake until two or three in the morning, my bony shoulders and butt painful on the wood floor, thinking about the new direction my road had taken. I heard Deb go to the bathroom after everybody was snoring, so I went over and waited until she came out, like I had to go next. She whispered, "Oh good, somebody else not sleeping," and we went into the bathroom together. She was wearing only an XL T-shirt that came down like a miniskirt. Her breasts moved beneath it, nipples showing through. I was so excited, I thought the guys out in the living room would hear my heart pounding. Deb and I both got the giggles and had to cover our mouths. I sat on the toilet and she sat on the edge of the tub.

We talked about Crete, about writing, the jazzers asleep on the floor. Soon we were yawning. We turned out the light and tiptoed back to our sleeping bags. A blizzard of feelings whirled in my glass ball of a brain.

I hitched over to Indianapolis the next day, and the deal went down just like Sgt. Rucker outlined it. They said my obligation to the Army had been extinguished and gave me a new reporting date two weeks away, meaning I could stay a few more days with Jim and Deb in Champaign.

Deborah and I and two guys went to see *Guess Who's Coming to Dinner?* We couldn't believe that preachers and rednecks across the country were trying to ban the movie because Sidney Poitier, the most handsome and polite black actor of the day, was dating a young white woman, a first for Hollywood. Every showing at the theatre where we saw it was packed. In the middle of the film, Deb and I leaned against each other as we were laughing. I took her hand, she looked at me and put her other hand over her mouth to stifle a laugh, but laced fingers with me.

For the rest of the time I was there, Deb and I stayed as close as we could. We'd all go to a pizza place, and she and I would sit together and do Mike Nichols and Elaine May comedy routines, parodies of awkward couples. The jazzers were into all kinds of improvisation, and sometimes we'd get into voices and satire scenes and everybody in the joint wound up staring at us as we raved on and on. Deborah was such a hoot — a wacky, stacked little fireball who held her own with all the speed-talkers in Jim's group.

It was hard to leave. I had come to say good-bye to Jim and with luck said hello to Deborah. She was off to meet their parents and fly to Crete. I was off to San Antonio for officer-training school. I felt like we'd see each other again. It sure cushioned the idea of military induction to have a crush on someone who was sort of in the military too.

I called my Dad to tell him the news, hoping he'd admire my discovery and praise my decision. "You got a ride hitchhiking, and you changed services? You believed the guy?" my dad said. "Isn't that a little erratic, son? Have you lost your mind?"

"No. I think it's a better deal, Dad."

"Good God, son. I don't know what to say."

"You wanted me to avoid Vietnam," I said.

"That's true, son. But you signed up for the Army, at a recruiting office."

"And now I'm signed up for the Air Force after a personal intervention by an Air Force recruiting coordinator." Silence from Dad, who hadn't served in WWII because he was married to my mom and had me and my sister, but now he knew all about what it meant to be drafted in 1967.

"I'll write you, Dad."

I also called my mom.

"Steve, remember: it's your country, right or wrong," she said. "Don't join those protesters. Or those … whatever they call themselves."

"Hippies, Mom?"

"Yes, them! Tearing down the country."

I gathered my stuff. Deb and a couple of jazzers came out on the porch with us. I shook hands with the guys. "Take care, man." I picked up my suitcase, which gave me something to do with one arm, and leaned down and put my other arm around her. "'Bye, Deb," I said, kissing her on the temple.

"Bye Famous Roommate."

# FOUR

In a window seat on an American Airlines flight, I was headed to Athens, Greece, on August 6, 1968. After nine months of communications officer school in Biloxi, Mississippi, I was finally on my way to reunite with Deborah in the fabled land whose history and mythology I had read so much about. Dozing, my head against a pillow resting on the plane's double-glass window as we crossed the Atlantic, I thought about what had got me to this point: months of basic training in the heat of San Antonio, where we were up at 5:30 to the amplified sound of a needle dropping onto a scratched vinyl recording of a bugle. We ate at 6:15 and ran a mile at 7:30. I'd lost twenty pounds off my skinny frame.

The stewardess (as we called them back then) on the flight to Greece woke me up to give me dinner on a tray. Fortunately, I'd gained back all the weight I'd lost in basic training. As I ate the airlines meal, complete with a glass of red wine, I thought about an epiphany I'd had halfway through officer school.

My training officer had called me into his office and said, "I'm assigning you to help train an incoming group. I know you'll do an outstanding job."

I soon spotted every weakness and deficiency among the new guys. I got impatient, I pushed and needled, I got sarcastic with them. And then one time, standing in the dorm hallway, I found myself raising my voice at them. They were jammed in a hallway like a small herd of sheep listening to me, their hands clasped in front of their crotches in their baggy boxer shorts.

A part of my mind rose out of my head like a mist and looked down on the scene. As I looked at my charges in that hallway, I changed. I had seen myself from an outside vantage point and I could no longer bully them. It scared me to see how easy it was to take my place on the ladder of hierarchy.

I said "dismissed" to them, and as they turned back down the hallway and peeled off into their dorm rooms, I felt amazed and grateful for my out-of-body insight, that I had caught myself being a militarist, and that compassion, not competition, was what I wanted to teach. We weren't being trained to carry rifles and grenades and protect each other in firefights. We had been uprooted from our lives and studies because of a war in Southeast Asia that nobody under-stood. Whether or not we were in Vietnam or combat, this war was grinding into all of us somehow or another.

Back at my room, I wondered if anyone in the new group had noticed my change in demeanor. Could it get back to my peers, or to my training officer? My superiors would consider my new outlook incompetent, insubordinate, maybe treasonous. So I told nobody and apparently nobody knew. It was an epiphany meant only for me.

The airline wine and turkey dinner made me drowsy. I leaned my seat back and again fell into reveries of the past year as we flew over a darkened Europe, bright ropes of freeway lights joining brilliant islands of city lights through holes in the clouds.

Deborah's last letter from Crete echoed in my mind. I'd reread it so many times I knew it by heart. *Dear Slender Lieutenant,* she began, her left-handed fountain pen spilling straight up-and-down cursive, with the o's and loops in wide ovals voluptuous, wide-eyed and open just like she was.

*Greetings from Knossos, the veritable lair of the Minotaur," she wrote. "I hope you've survived Lack-Land* [Lackland Air Base] *in one piece. You're quite close to my last asylum, Our Lady of the Lake. The Land of Lack and Lady of the Lake are similar, actually. Sister campuses of The Holy Family of Hierarchical Control. My dad was stationed there, you know. I ran around San Antonio with my girlfriend Loretta Guerra.*

*I don't know whether this letter will reach you. I'm knockin' back some ouzo and praying to the blue sea that it will. I and my books are cozy in my tiny bedroom in the parents' place in base housing; Kazantzakis, Lawrence Durrell, and the poet Cavafy keep me company.*

*Our few days together at Q-mo's (what I call my brother Jim's) were a blast. The parents are a little too tired to tie me down, so I'm ramblin'. There are many cool guys here on this base — linguists listening in on Mediterranean radio and telephone traffic, spies, dopers. Some wear bell-bottoms and don't even shave. They can't be disciplined for "personal grooming" because their language skills are so valuable.*

*But there's nobody I can talk books with like you. Are you really a lieutenant now? How weird! I can't imagine you in the Air Force. Do you have anybody to talk to? You should come here! Iraklion Base is by the capital of Crete and my dad's a wheel on base.*

*Sheep and goats with copper bells walk down the highways. Lots of people look like me! I blend in. Cafés on every corner in town. Ouzo tastes like licorice, wine tastes like rusted horse piss but gets you so mellow you can try to speak Greak. Or is it speek Greek? Consumables of every kind for the head, an international hippie colony across the island at Matala — free flights to Athens every few hours for us USAF dependents.*

*You won't believe the Palace of Knossos and the Minoan pottery! I used to think Christ was old school, but these guys were flipping over bulls 1,600 years before that! I will send you a brochure I purloined from the museum today. It would be a gas to share exploring this place with you. I need somebody to talk Durrell and Kazantzakis with.*

*Take care and write me at the APO address on the envelope if you read something good. I may be gallivanting about Europe but they'll forward or hold letters for me. Think there's any chance you'll get sent over here?*

*Your fellow pilgrim among the imperialists, Deborah.*

As our plane banked into the sunrise over Athens, I saw there were no tall buildings. The white cubist city sprawled over a plain between mountains and the sea. There were two tall spots — one a mini Mt. Fuji with a white church at its top, and the other, I was thrilled to see, was a white mesa with the famous Parthenon temple on it. Everything else seemed to be only four or five stories high. We landed at a big airport at the edge of the sea, the old Athenai Airport, destined to be demolished in the 1980s.

I walked from the plane to the terminal, inhaling new smells: the brine of the ocean wind from the west and a mix of lemon sweetness and meat cooking from somewhere close. My stomach tingled: *I have landed in legendary Greece!* As I walked out of the baggage-claim area into Athens, savory smoke from a food vendor's cart on the sidewalk shot into my nostrils. The vendor grinned widely, one of a long line of benign Greek traveler-predators, especially on the lookout for U.S. Air Force personnel arriving from abroad.

"What is that?" I asked, pointing to green-speckled and sizzling meat in a spicy cloud.

"Ka-bob," he said. "Chicken!"

"What are the spices?"

"Thymari!" he said, spreading his hands and raising his eyebrows. "Romero!" Then in English for me, "Thyme! Rose-mari!" The guy looked like a 1940s' romantic film star — pencil mustache, bold chin, wavy salt-and-pepper hair in a pompadour, boat captain's cap on the back of his head. So I didn't miss the intended effect, he pointed to a black-and-white publicity photo taped to his menu board. The caption read "Tyrone Power in *The Mark of Zorro.*" He turned his profile to match the photo and said, "Eh? Like me? Vassilis is Tyrone!"

I was cramped and queasy after the long flight from New York and wasn't hungry, but he was such a welcoming ambassador, I walked away from Tyrone Power's souvlaki cart with a kabob. I turned and looked at the glittering sea I'd just flown over. *This is the sea Homer spoke of, that Odysseus sailed, that Athens ruled,* I thought. I was giddy in my historical reverie. I asked the first cabbie in line at the taxi stand to take me to "Athenai Base, American Air Force."

He grinned and pointed behind me. "It's just there," he said. "You could walk."

I looked where he was pointing, and there were tall triangular tails of C-130 cargo planes showing above the top of a huge chain-link fence at the south end of Athenai Airport. As I got in the cab, the driver lit up a cigarette and said, "Okay, I take you to the base." We zoomed onto Vouliagmenis Boulevard and took the next right into Athenai Base, a 30-second ride.

The security guy at the guard shack stared into the cab and then saluted the gold bars on the collar of my uniform shirt. The first thing we passed after the guard shack was a regulation-size baseball diamond. *Little America,* I thought. *Play ball!* I used to enjoy being a good third baseman in city-league softball. But I hadn't come here to play ball.

Inside a plain one-story building was my outfit, the 2140th Comm Squadron, my new home for the next three years. I went in, taking off my cap. An attractive middle-aged Greek woman with short waved black hair, dark eyeliner and blue eye shadow took me to the door of my new commander, Colonel Bert Fisher. He was tall and thin, with reddish hair combed straight back. He smiled as I came into his office, stood and came around his desk.

"Reporting for duty, sir," I said.

"Welcome to Athenai Base, Lieutenant. Glad to have you. I understand there's going to be some wedding bells in your future, Stephen. Is that right?"

"Yes, sir," I answered, smiling broadly. *We'll cross that bridge when we get to it,* I thought. *It's just a little white lie — nothing like the ones the Pentagon and Army recruiters told us about Vietnam. I hope Sergeant Cuomo doesn't get wind that Deborah is my "fiancée."* When I'd left Communications Officer school at Biloxi, Mississippi, where the Air Force security snoops were punishing my two best officer friends for giving talks at the Unitarian Church, it seemed to me that telling the Communications Command that Deb was my fiancée was the best way to assure that I could get to Greece to spend time with her. To my surprise and joy, they bought it and found a slot for me in Greece.

"Well, we're glad to be a part of a wedding. Sit down," the colonel said in his soft voice, pulling a chair close to the desk. "We don't have an active slot for you, Steve, but we said we'd take you early and figure something out."

Fisher was friendly, gentle and well educated. "We think it would be good for you to learn your way around our outlying detachments by taking over the CIUWF — the Central Isolated Unit Welfare Fund. It's how we finance hobby activities for the men at our fifteen remote detachments. And some of them are *really* remote, across Greece on mountaintops. We ask them what they want and try to accommodate them. We'll give you a car and driver. Should take about four or five weeks to visit all ten "dets," as we call them, meet the site commanders, get their views of what the men need — books, records, more films, whatever. My feeling is that it's better to spring for a custom darkroom setup than to have to bail 'em out of jail or pay child support to a local gal's family."

*Wow. They want me to tour the country before I start work, because they took me early? My luck continues!*

Fisher called out to his secretary to bring us a couple of coffees.

"To give you an idea of what we do here," he went on, "we're the southeast flank of NATO. You studied NATO at officer school, right?"

"No sir, not much. Basically, it's Western Europe, isn't it?"

The colonel told me that NATO now runs from Norway to the edge of Iraq. All the communications from around the Mediterranean, from the U.S. and NATO bases in Norway, to England, Spain, Germany, France, Italy — all of it — come into Greece at the Mount Pateras site. He pointed to western Greece on the map. "It gets relayed through the other sites to Salonika," he swept the pointer over to northeastern Greece and down to the entrance to the Black Sea, "then into Turkey and down into Israel. Well, you're not supposed to know that. Israel isn't a NATO country. Don't ever mention that to people here in Athens. Or to your family back in the States. That's security clearance stuff. Our broadband carries everything from our in-country telephone lines to our top-secret encrypted NATO communications," he said.

I tried to remember my instruction in encryption at the Biloxi Comm Officer school. All I could remember was stealing the carved wooden "Security" insignia from the Biloxi base's security vault and taking it back to the apartment I shared with another two lieutenants. My first act of civil disobedience.

"We're not tourists here, Steve," Colonel Fisher was saying. "Greece is bordered on the north, as I'm sure you know, by *communist regimes* — Albania, Bulgaria, Yugoslavia. Turkey, to the east, might as well be a Muslim country, even though they prefer to be called a secular republic. We're aware that Turkey may be susceptible to manipulation by the countries that border it to the north — all Soviet states with large Muslim populations — as well as their other bordering countries, Iran, Iraq and Syria. Our mission is to know what's going on in this little hot spot of the earth. To help NATO hold the line against volatile regimes — the communists to the north, Muslims to the east. Whatever threatens the Free World."

On the map behind Fisher's head I could see Greece's intricate coastlines, its many islands dotting the Mediterranean right up to Turkey's coast, and its equally jagged northern borders with those countries he'd mentioned were either Communist or Muslim. In my mind, those countries were blank, far more remote than anything in Greece.

Colonel Fisher continued, "There's a letter in your file about your helping local adults with literacy back there in Mississippi. Were they Negro? I think that's wonderful, helping the community. Congratulations, Stephen."

The colonel leaned back in his creaky chair, appearing relaxed with me. "So what we'll be counting on, Steve, is hearing from you weekly on exactly how those channels on our broadband stream — about 57 of them, at last count — are performing, day to day. We can't afford any outages, any interference, any message corruption."

"Yes, sir. Of course," I said, setting my little coffee cup on its little saucer. Of course I had no clue. I was jet-lagged from the long flight and most of what he said had been a blur. If he weren't so pleasant and didn't seem so genuinely nice, I might've felt the chill of dread lock around me. Instead, I thought, *Well, I'm not the first raw lieutenant to be in this position. I was a distinguished graduate of OTS. I made A's at Comm School. Let's just assume that it won't be any harder than that.*

Colonel Fisher took me around and introduced me to my direct supervisor, Captain Al Citron, dark and handsome like Tony Bennett, who punctuated his conversation by pausing to search for just the right word, making little circles with his upheld forefinger. Al introduced me to the rest of the people in our three rooms of offices and then took me to lunch with the real bosses of the outfit, a chief master sergeant about five-foot-five with bulging tattooed arms, and Senior Master Sergeant Bobby Land, who had his hair slicked up into fenders over his ears like a fifties rockabilly star.

"I'll brief you on all of our operations whenever you're ready, Lieutenant," said Bobby Land. "Just don't touch any of the equipment, if you don't mind," he added.

*No, I don't mind that at all.*

"Just a couple of warnings for you, Steve," said Fisher when I looked into his office after lunch. "There's a lady we call the Glyfada Gobbler you want to avoid. Don't ever stop to talk with her. And there's a street you want to avoid also, Bouboulinas Street, where the National Archaeology Museum is."

I wondered what would be the threat of the museum of archaeology — *the very place I looked forward to seeing* — and a woman who
sounded like a turkey? I told him archaeology was one reason I was
glad to be in Greece. He told me that there was a police station near
there and sometimes you could hear screaming.

"Welcome to Greece, Lieutenant," he concluded. "Take a few
days to find a house to rent, then report to Captain Citron. You're
welcome to take a hop across to Crete to visit your fiancée's family. It's
a little over an hour away. Our cargo planes go several times a day.
Nice to have you with us."

I saluted, he did a quick return salute, then shook my hand and
turned back to his desk. I walked out of his office thinking, *This guy
Fisher isn't bad. I wonder: has he ever met a communist? Or a Muslim?
Will I?*

# FIVE

I'd often wondered what kind of house I would live in when I got to Greece. I'd hoped that it would be a whitewashed bungalow. Something austere and vernacular, like the photo of Leonard Cohen's house on the island of Hydra that was on the back cover of his poetry book, *The Spice-Box of Earth*. I bought that book before leaving the States, because Cohen had just appeared on the music scene, in April 1967, and the island he lived on, Hydra, was not far from Athens. I thought I might get to meet him. The first track on his debut album was "Susanne." Everyone was talking about it, and I was intrigued by the line, "You know that she's half crazy but that's why you want to be there." Something about that line made me muse about Deborah. On the back cover of the album was a woman surrounded by flames. *Was she in Johnny Cash's Ring of Fire? Was she dying or transcending?* The album didn't say.

The house I found through the listings at Base Housing wasn't Leonard's adobe-looking poet's retreat: it was white, but it had a red tile roof and a wide shady porch. A five-foot white masonry wall enclosed the front yard, which was a lush garden of orange trees and ancient rose bushes blooming in red, orange, and yellow.

"I am Mr. Petros," the landlord said in a heavy accent and husky voice. "Come, come, leftenant," he said, taking me gently by the elbow, with an old man's courtesy. He pronounced the "u" in lieutenant as an "f," as Greeks did all u's. Odysseus, for example, was pronounced "Odyssefs." That made me take notice of all the ways in which Greek might be different than I thought.

"Everything here, for to be nice," said Mr. Petros, sweeping his arm in a wide arc. It was the first of several phrases he used repeatedly in his heartfelt but limited English. He took me through the house. With its polished terrazzo floors and huge framed posters of Greek islands rearing up out of the sea, it was nicer than any house my parents had ever had, or anywhere I'd ever lived. He wrote the rent on a piece of paper: 400 drachmas. A drachma was twenty-five cents, one U.S. quarter, in those days. When I did the math in my head I could hardly believe it: he was renting me this lovely house for $100 a month! With my housing allowance and overseas pay I was making $480 a month. I gave him a check from my new checking account and we shook hands. This was my first insight into the gulf between the American economy and this tiny country of six or seven million and their funny-sized bills in pastel colors with kings wearing military epaulets and medals. I was instantly rich, for the first time in my life.

I called Air Operations on the base and asked about a flight to Iraklion Air Base on Crete. There was one leaving in an hour, the last hop of the day, so I took it. The DC-3 flew south from Athens, out over the Aegean Sea toward Crete, the largest Greek island, the home of the legendary Minoans. We flew over smaller islands rocky and steep, spaced like stepping stones across the Aegean.

"That's Crete ahead of us, Lieutenant," one of the pilots called back through the roar. "Come on up and take a look."

With a hand on the back of each of their seats, I looked between the pilots out through the plane's slanted and bug-splatted windshield. Crete, King Minos and his Minotaur! The pottery Deb had sent me pictures of! We could see all the way across the island to the sea that continued rolling on to North Africa. In a few minutes we approached the north shoreline at the edge of a broad bay with a city spreading away from it. The coast had a thin line of white surf blinking on and off as waves hit. Tiny boats trailing wakes made Vs close to the shore.

"How big is Crete?" I yelled.

"About 150 miles long, maybe 60 miles wide at the widest. Better strap in, we're comin' in pretty hot. Gonna bank hard here in a minute."

I went back and knelt down in front of the first cabin window, bracing myself against a bulkhead. As we banked to the right into the westerly wind and lost altitude, I sucked up the sights below. The sea was bluer than any sea I'd ever imagined. It was liquid lapis.

"Right over Iraklion, buddy," yelled the pilot. We hit some bouncy air and I whacked my head on the fuselage wall curving up over me. Rebracing myself, I could see we were completing a U-turn into a tiny air base east of Iraklion.

I called Chief Master Sergeant Dominic Cuomo's residence from Air Ops, and in ten more minutes there was Deborah, a smile lighting up her face, with her dad, who was not much taller than she was, walking stiffly beside her. I wanted to sweep her up in a hug but didn't. Her father, whom she spoke of as Dom, had a buzz-cut formality, the huge display of stripes of the highest enlisted rank lining each arm from shoulder to elbow. I stuck out my hand. He snapped me a salute instead. Oh, right — I was an officer and he had to salute me first. I felt embarrassed to — technically — outrank such a career man.

Facing this steely little guy, I saluted back, after which he kindly extended his hand and we shook, a smile spreading across his face.

"Welcome, Steve," he said. "Great to meet you."

Just that smoothly, he slipped past the military protocol to the role of a father whose two young adult children were my closest friends. He had a great hawk nose and probing eyes — Jim and Deb did not inherit those eyes; they must have got their big, liquid artist's eyes from their mom. He was about five-four, with gray shining at the temples and on his forearms. He reminded me of the two senior sergeants running my squadron back in Athens, both short and impressive men.

Deb was wearing a pink sleeveless sundress, miniskirt length, a bright-yellow bra showing through the armholes. She told me later that she and a girlfriend had dyed their underwear just for the hell of it, to push back against the military's dress codes and behavior standards. I was a little surprised by how short she was and wondered what Dom thought of the ironic, playful quality of her smile. I felt butterflies in my gut. I bore down to keep my elation under control, seeing her after more than a year and all the avid letters that had passed between us.

Dom drove us into the base-housing area. Their house had a bit of lawn around it and some flowers. Waiting at the door was Deb's mother, Lucia, the same height as Deb but wider. Inside, I saw she had decorated the living and dining area of the house with doilies, religious icons, Bible verses and lots of framed pictures of family, including the Pope, every Catholic's father. The two younger children — David, an appealing little kid of about seven with sticks for arms and legs, and eleven-year-old Cathie, who had wavy hair and a wary look — came out to meet me.

One of the framed photos on the wall was a picture of Lucia,

clipped from a newspaper, when JFK and Jackie had visited San
Antonio on the Texas trip before going on to Dallas. Jackie was
leaning down to greet Lucia and David, who were looking up at the
First Lady. The photo appeared in the San Antonio paper the next day,
as did other photos of the catastrophe in Dallas, two days after that
sweet moment between two mothers adoring a young child. I was
moved by this photo that reminded me of that terrible day in 1963 in
my hometown. And the photo also warmed my heart toward the
Cuomo family. Jackie seemed to be giving a blessing to Lucia and her
young boy, who was about the same age as her little John-John, and to
their Catholic family.

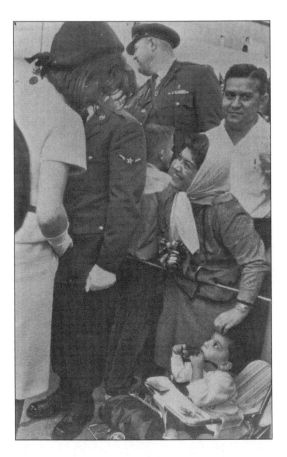

While the kids went back to their rooms and Deb helped her mom with the dinner, Dom excused himself and changed into some slacks and a pressed sport shirt. He invited me to sit with him in the small living room, he in an easy chair and I on a sofa across a coffee table from him. He talked proudly about his son Jim's career in jazz, which seemed to be taking off, and showed me a new album by The Flock, a Chicago jazz/rock group. The band's picture on the vinyl album cover showed them with long hair past their shoulders.

For a second, I thought he was going to disparage their wild look. Instead, he said, "Now these guys're excellent musicians. Jimmy's played with them. They're not like these rock and rollers — they know jazz." In one way I marveled that my ultra-hip friend Jim had come from this pious and regimented family. But as I talked with Dom, I saw how intelligent he was and that he'd been through some deep maturing process in his Air Force life. His pride in Jim touched me.

When Lucia called out that dinner was ready, Dom said grace as they all bowed their heads. With bowls of pasta and meat sauce, corn, and salad, I filled up, and Deb and I managed to keep the polite ping-pong of conversation going with only a couple of "help us!" looks at each other.

Over after-dinner coffee, Dom put some swinging Sinatra on the record player with those big-band Nelson Riddle arrangements. I asked what he did, and he told me, "I can't really tell you. But you know this is a security base. In Air Force parlance that means intelligence. You've got a top-secret clearance. But there are several levels above that. I'm sure the Comm Officer course gave you a little background, enough to get the picture anyway. We're in touch with your Comm squadron in Athens every week if need be, and daily, of course, with the intelligence squadron at Athenai."

Deb had told me in one of her letters that the mandatory retirement age, according to the regulations then in force, was after thirty years of service. Dom was in his thirty-third year with no whispers of retirement. Deb said that meant he was too important to be let go. I was skittish about entering the circle of such a veteran intelligence guy. There was a tricky side to the bargain Deb had made by coming here with her family. She was leading a double life right under the nose of a canny old spy.

Back at the visiting officers' dorm, after the evening at the Cuomos', I was the only guest. In the late evening I smoked a piece of hash Deborah had slipped me. It was wrapped in a note: "Tomorrow I'll show you Knossos." I wandered out across the small base to the National Road that ran along the coast, then headed east up this road, pleasantly ripped, a pilgrim in jeans out to meet something of Greece, this fabled land. At a little bay, with the full moon coming up out of the sea and waves rolling onto the rocky shore, I sat on a rock, zonked. My brain churned out some metaphysical insights: *Yes… the visible,*

*mechanical energy of these waves turn into sound as they hit the shore, and the sound waves radiate out. We who hear them turn them into <u>thought</u> energy... so energy is, in fact, a continuum. Aha!* Around midnight a villager appeared and kindly walked me back to the base. Apparently, if I understood him right, it wasn't Homer's seashore I had been standing on, but this man's backyard.

* * *

A knocking sound slowly penetrated my dream. A voice was speaking English. It was a two-syllable word. Someone was repeating it. It was "Stevie." *Oh, that's me.*

"Stevie! Get up, it's me." I let Deborah in. "Oooh-h-h," she chortled. "Good walk last night?"

All I could do was nod and grin. The Cuomos had gone to early mass with the kids, and Deborah told them she was going to sleep in. She sure took her chances with them. I pulled on some jeans and a polo shirt, and we took a base bus into town, a fifteen-minute ride along the coast. She told me I had done a great job at the family dinner last night, and I told her she did, too, and thanks for that dynamite little hash present.

"It's everywhere over here," she said. "I'm sure Dom and the base commander have decided hash is just like alcohol, it keeps the troops cooled out and with much less fighting and dormitory destruction." Of course I told her about my little excursion down the National Road, with my mystical insights.

"You risk-taker, you!" she said. "But you found out that the Greek villagers are just as sweet as they can be. I've never had any bad situations. And I've been all over."

After an American-style breakfast at a taverna on the highway, we took a taxi to the other end of the breakwater. We climbed up the old walls the Venetians had built. Deb was wearing brown bell-bottom jeans and a Mexican-style white blouse with elastic at the top that could be a scooped neckline or stretch out over the shoulders.

"Nice," I said.

"San Antonio," she grinned. "My Mexicana look."

I admired her gameness and agility as we climbed. At the top, we had an exhilarating view of the Mediterranean. In a paved area overlooking the city was the grave of Nikos Kazantzakis, the Cretan who became Greece's greatest writer. The grave was covered with a massive slab of granite, with a tall cross of thin wood at the head.

"What a beautiful spot, eh?" she said. "Check out the epitaph." She translated, "I hope for nothing. I fear nothing. I am free." Deb had been reading up on Kazantzakis and told me that he had died and been buried here only ten years earlier. As a young man, he had tried to work in the coal mines on Crete — he wasn't good enough — but down in the mine he met a Macedonian named Yorgos Zorbas, full of life, humor, irony and defiance.

We sat on a bench under the shade of a diminutive windblown tree. She took a bottle of water out of her pack. I said that I remembered a quote from the book: Zorba says, "the greatest sin is not to sleep with a woman when the chance is offered."

"Great line," she said. We had both seen the film *Zorba the Greek* twice in the last year, with Alan Bates as the Kazantzakis character and Anthony Quinn as Zorba. I was trying to suggest to myself by quoting that line that I would be up to the opportunity, so to speak, when the situation presented itself. I was so clueless about intercourse, wondering how I could be the initiator of it, as the male role seemed to stipulate, when I knew so little about female anatomical details and what women wanted. If you just asked them about those things, would that mean you were laughably clueless? I just had to hope that some miracle of grace would happen. I wanted to talk with Deb about it — break my own silence and see what she thought — but I couldn't overcome my fears. I was frustrated with my passivity. I worried. I hoped I'd grow out of it. I longed to be like Zorba.

We took the bus back to the base. At lunch with the family, I saw how much Deb loved her little brother, David. I watched as she avidly drank in his jerky movements and goofy child's chatter. He took up his sandwich and peered into it, naming the ingredients and snorting at the words.

"Lettuce. Let us what? Let us eat? OK, we're eating! Mustard. We must do what? We must eat! Ummm, turkey. Well ..."

Lucia shushed him and asked me how I'd enjoyed the walk with her daughter.

I said the Kazantzakis grave was at a gorgeous spot. She said that Deb really liked his writing, but she herself hadn't read him. "Too busy raising a family," she said. I felt some empathy for her in her role as a military wife, going wherever her husband was assigned, and as a Catholic mom of her era, raising the kids, never working or taking trips on her own. I wondered what her and Dom's marriage was like. Already, it was obvious that Deb was diverging from that pattern, as I was from my parents', politically and culturally, as the events of the sixties changed the landscape that had shaped the older generation. Jim, Deb and I were on a different planet from theirs.

Deb announced to the parents that she was going to show me the ruins of Knossos, the palace of the Minoans.

"I'll go! I'll go! Please, Debbie!" David said, forgetting his sandwich. Lucia suggested we take him along, but Deb said we'd be climbing too much rough stuff and going too fast for him.

We rode the bus into town again and, at the station by the harbor, took the Knossos bus that went inland along the eastern edge of town. I was looking forward to seeing the Knossos ruins, not only because their art, in the brochure Deb had sent me, had that flowing water-and-wave quality of art I'd seen in Biloxi, but also because they were about a thousand years older than the Athens ruins. The kings of Knossos used to rule the whole eastern Mediterranean.

The myths about the place were old and tangled with later Athenian versions, but they went something like this: Zeus, who was called the father of all the other gods and of heroic humans, seduced Europa (whom we remembered to call Ev-ropa), the daughter of the king of Phoenicia (now known as Venice, Italy). Evropa gave birth to a child they called Minos, who was raised by the king of Crete. When the king died, Minos took over; the story goes that a woman or nymph got very physically attracted to a white bull Poseidon had given Minos. She was so smitten that she had a wooden cow made. The bull got hot for the cow, so, secreting herself inside the wooden cow, this woman got pregnant by the amorous bull (what a picture!). The result was a man/bull hybrid they called the Minotaur. Minos kept this unusual creature in a maze underneath the palace, where Minos conducted foreign policy by making captives face the Mino-taur in one-on-one battles.

"Ahhhhh! It's worse than the Bible!" I told Deb as we tried to follow the mythology at the entrance to the Knossos ruins. "There are no walls between the gods, the nymphs and the humans!"

"I know," Deb said, "No walls between history, religion, archae-ology, metaphor and archetype, either!"

We cackled in delighted exasperation.

I thought to myself, *This could keep my mind off Vietnam and civil rights for a while. The thousand-year soap opera behind Western Civilization!*

The ruins were on a low hill where two streams came together.

Much of the site was just outlines of now-vanished walls, but tile-mosaic floors were still there, only six inches beneath the soil, they say, when Sir Arthur Evans began digging for it. It is considered Europe's oldest city, so there was tremendous buzz about it among archaeologists. Several blocks of restored rooms stuck up here and there. Obviously they had been restored, because they were now painted bright red and blue, their surfaces perfectly smooth, and whole walls of decorative paintings had been generated from little patches of the original frescoes.

Deb said, "Let's visit these restorations then go see the museum, where the good stuff is, at least the stuff Athens hasn't hauled off to its National Museum."

One reconstructed part was called the Hall of the Double Axes, with a double ax carved on many of the stones. *Ahh, the dark side of empire. The weapons of the day. As if the Minotaur wasn't dark enough.*

"These axes were obviously not garden tools," I said.

"Right! Axe me what they mean," she said.

"Okay, I'm axin' ya."

"So the Greek word for ax is *labrys*. With these things carved all over this part of the palace, all jumbled up, it turned into our word labyrinth. Intricate maze. Ta da!"

"I'm certainly amazed, I don't know about you," I said in a TV detective voice.

We were facing one restoration, with a row of red columns, larger at the top and tapering to the bottom, holding up a piece of roof over a plastered wall with a mural on it. Deb announced, "Stevie, there's hardly anybody here at this time of day. I'm gonna duck behind this wall here, and I need you to stay here. If anyone comes, cough real loud." I guessed she needed to pee. I kept watch, looking up and down the pathway. I heard a "pssst" and turned back toward the portico. Deb was standing in front of the throne in a heroic pose, her boobs sticking right out over the elastic neckline of her Mexican blouse.

My jaw dropped, I'm sure, as I stared in disbelief. She had pulled a Gypsy-style purple-and-green skirt over her jeans. She made a full turn, a fake hair fall flowing down her back, both arms held out with wiggly "snakes" made of what looked like copper wire. Then I got it! She was burlesquing the postcard she'd sent me of the most famous — or notorious — image of Knossos, its bare-breasted "snake goddess." The archaeologists had argued over whether or not it was a forgery, while tourists and history buffs discreetly appreciated the chance to study a topless costumed lady. I hooted as I got it. It was the first scene I'd ever seen that was funny and sexy and a parody of art history all at the same time. Deb shushed me and then we heard voices down the path. She snapped her elastic neckline up and slipped back behind the wall. I walked toward the voices to stall them. I asked them if they had a map of the ruins and discovered they were Brits. "Right-o," a man said. I fumbled with the map, asking some inane question till Deb appeared behind them, the snakes, fall and skirt apparently stuffed back into her pack.

As we walked away I said, "Jesus, Deb. Where'd you get that stuff?"

"The base thrift shop and the flea market in town. My buddies in electronics made the snakes out of wiring harnesses. I knew it would blow your mind."

"You really know this place," I said. "You went down one way and came around the other."

"Comes from hours of avoiding the family. I know every path and escape route in Knossos. And in Iraklion."

"Intrepid!" I said in British accent.

"You need to be when you live with a spy on a military base," she said. "Or just if you deal with nuns and priests all your life."

She and her brother, Jim, were smart recovering Catholics, like many others I admired and became friends with. We reached the museum walkway and sat down on a bench.

"Well, I wanted to bring the old mythology alive for my lieutenant," she said.

"You sure did that," I said. "And may I say, great boobs."

"Those Italian genes come in handy. When you got 'em, flaunt 'em," she said. "But…" She looked away.

"What?"

"Anyway. Nothing."

"Tell me."

"I could only do that for you because it was funny. Try being mistaken for twelve all the time by 'normal' people but have sergeants as old as your father stare at your chest. Then let your mother see you naked and go, 'Oh my God, Deborah!' Big boobs are not fun in my experience. For females, something's always wrong." We sat in silence while I tried to process that.

"It's a tall world, Stevie, and I'm on the short end of it. At least here in Greece, I don't stand out as much." This was the first time we had broached the topic of height.

"Wow. Being the height I am, I know I can't appreciate what it feels like."

"I know," she said. "You'd have to be a ball boy for the Lakers or something. But look around. There are lots of people here not much taller than me. It's a huge relief not hearing inane comments."

"To me, Deb, you're just cool. You're beyond height."

"Beyond height!" she hooted. "Hobbit From Another Dimension!" She stuck out her chest. "Get back, men, Amazon comin' through!" We both laughed, then got up and went into the museum. I scooped my arm around her shoulder, she put her arm around my butt, her thumb hooked in my jeans back pocket, and we slowed our walk.

There were lots of little treasures in the museum, but we'd both had enough for the day. We went back down the Knossos hill and waited at the bus stop.

"Debórah," I said, putting the emphasis on the middle syllable and creating a private name I could use for her, "I've been waiting for this day for over a year. It's so great to be here with you." She said ditto for her.

"But uh…this morning at the taverna I noticed a couple of guys looking at you like they knew you…like, pretty well." I asked her if one of them was a boyfriend of hers.

"No. They're just a couple of guys I'd hang out with, score hash with, escape the family with. Nobody like you."

It took me a long time to ask the question that seemed to hang in the air.

"You slept together?"

She kept her eyes straight ahead. "With one. Just once. The blond one. His name is Wart."

"Wart? Nice name."

Anyway, she said, she didn't want me to get weirded out if Wart saw us and made some crack about it.

I stared straight ahead too. *Well,* I thought, *at least she's not trying to hide it.* She said he was a macho guy and she did it to lose her virginity. Get that out of the way. That was a goal of mine, too, in joining the service. Couldn't get too crazy over that. But I *was* jealous. *When's it going to happen for me?* I wondered. *And "Wart?" Hop into bed with a fungus!*

I squeezed her close, turned my face and kissed her on the temple.

"Okay then. I hope Dom hasn't heard about how I got sent over here. The 'fiancée' thing." She said he hadn't heard, she was sure.

\* \* \*

We caught the bus heading back, got off at the center of Iraklion and walked to a hub called Lion's Square. The town's major streets radiated out from this spot. It looked like there wasn't a right-angle intersection in all of Heraklion. It was still kind of a labyrinth.

Deb said, "Let's find a café. I need to talk to you."

*Uh-oh. When somebody says that, it's usually something serious you don't want to hear.* As we looked at the cafés, Deb took my hand. That was reassuring. We were on Dedalou Street, named for Daedalus, the guy who designed the maze for Minos and made wings for his son Icarus, who flew too close to the sun. The present, the past, the myth, the history, the metaphors, all interwoven here.

These cafés on Dedalou all specialized in a flaky pastry called bougatsas, filled with cheese or honey. We slipped into the shade of a portal and took a little white wrought-iron table. A waiter brought our coffees and bougatsas. Perched on the chair across from me, she looked twelve again, feet not hitting the ground, elbows on the table.

Sipping from my coffee to hide my mouth, I looked at her brown eyes, hoping it wasn't bad news. She sounded uncertain again, her voice going up at the end of each sentence. She told me about the college extension classes she'd been taking, here on Crete and at the University of Maryland campus in Munich, and that they'd gone so well that something unexpected had happened.

"I've been accepted by the American University in Paris. They've offered me a scholarship. I've got to go in a few days." A trap door fell open in my chest. She said, "There's this guy, Philippe, I met in Munich? He's from Paris? He's a photographer. He's giving me a place to stay." I stared at her. The noise of people walking by and cars passing was muffled. She reached out a hand to my arm.

"He's not a boyfriend. He's an old guy. He's disabled. He went through those riots in Paris? He photographed it? He prints photos for Cartier-Bresson, too."

*She knows somebody who knows Henri Cartier-Bresson? My photographic idol?* The traffic noise was so distant. I listened to the blood beating in my eardrums. She said it was just for one semester, then she'd be back here.

"After that, I'll probably go back to the States with the parents." She saw my dismay. "Listen: It's the American University in Paris. I'll never have a chance like this again. You and my insane brother, you already have your college. I don't. I can't pass this up!"

I called on my voice to say something, anything, to cover up my acute disappointment and my fear of losing her before I had a chance to know her. *Did I make up a mutual romance out of her letters, one that she didn't feel?* I stared out at the street.

"No, Deb. Sure, you can't pass this up." A moment went by. I was stunned. "So, the French guy, Phillipe. Be straight with me. You're not…with him, or anything?"

"No! Stevie, he's a smack freak. He does heroin. He's not very healthy. He's willing to teach me how to print black-and-white and show me where all the barricades were in Paris during the riots. That's *all*. Stevie, you know how I feel about you! I just showed you my boobs."

I wasn't sure what heroin or seeing boobs was proof of. And no, I wasn't sure how she felt about me.

"He's a smack freak who prints for Cartier-Bresson? You can do that on heroin?"

"He has a 'maintenance habit'," Deb explained, putting quote marks around it. "He can function. He says Cartier-Bresson just drops off twenty rolls at a time at this photo-finishing shop and doesn't ask them to do anything special. Stevie, it's really about school, photography and living in Paris for a semester. By the time you learn your way around Athens, I'll be back, and you can show me what you've discovered. I've never hung out in Athens."

The last rays of the sun came straight down the cobbled street in front of our coffee shop, and people crossing the street trailed long shadows three times their height. I didn't know what to say. This was such a huge disappointment. I paid our bill and we walked toward the bus station. Deb said that her snake-goddess caper was a royal send-off, so I'd have something to remember and look forward to.

"I'm sorry this is happening. But I'll be coming through Athens in two days," she said, brightening, "and we can spend the day together," she said.

"It does sound like a hell of an adventure. Those don't come along very often." I swallowed hard and stared straight ahead. "But you know I'm floored, Deb. I've been waiting to be with you for a year. I lied to the Air Force that you were the reason."

"Stevie. I'll come back for Christmas in four months. You're the one I'll want to see then."

We zigzagged around triangle-shaped blocks, holding our pinky fingers. Noisy Vespas, smoking motorbikes and rattly Fiat cabs barreled past on the bigger streets. The traffic flowed up onto the wide sidewalks, as both cars and motor scooters parked at all angles over the curb and pedestrian ways. Our ride to the base was quiet and distracted. I was sliding into a mood. I couldn't help it. This had complicated my feelings toward her, to say the least.

At the Cuomo house, I said good-bye to her parents. They invited me back for some upcoming Greek holiday. I shook hands with Dom, gave Lucia a hug and Deb a peck on the cheek and went to wait for the last hop of the day back to Athens. My feelings toward Deborah were so scrambled, and the landscape so unfamiliar and so vast, that I couldn't get my footing. I took the seat nearest a window in the cargo plane and studied the cobalt sea and the tiny boats trailing Vs of foam as the plane droned back to Athens.

# SIX

Two days after leaving the Cuomo family, on the morning of August 10th, I was at my desk at the Athens Communications Squadron. Having a new desk with a nameplate and a phone and some private space, even though two of the walls were just partitions, gave me a home base after nearly a year in the Air Force without a space of my own. My mind was divided and my emotions were jumpy as I sat putting pens, paper clips, and staples in the main drawer, and paper, folders and Isolated Unit Welfare Fund records in the file drawers. My first assignment would be to travel to all of our isolated detachments to see what the men in these remote places wanted from the squadron to help them pass the time.

Marlina, Colonel Fisher's secretary, had put a dish of Greek hard candies and a small vase of flowers on my desk, and people from the squadron kept dropping by to shake hands and welcome me. I asked Marlina, "Are you positive the phone on my desk has been activated? This was the day Deborah was supposed to come through Athens." Now that I knew I wouldn't be seeing her until Christmas, today's visit with her meant a lot to me.

"Oh yes, Lieutenant, we have tested it," she assured me.

When the phone rang, I snatched it up. It was Deborah.

"Steve, I'm coming on the 11 o'clock hop. Is that too soon?"

"Deborah! No, I'll meet you at Air Ops." My heart was thumping.

"Can you still spend the day with me?" she asked.

"We're on," I said. I told her I had cleared it with my commander that I could take her to lunch and take the afternoon off. I explained to him that Deborah had been surprised by a last-minute scholarship award to the American University in Paris, and that the Cuomos and I agreed she couldn't afford to pass it up.

He had said, "Of course. You two enjoy the day."

I had been scouring the tourist brochures and posters in the base exchange to see where I might take Deb this afternoon. It had to be special. I didn't know what there was within driving distance. At the BX travel desk, there were spectacular travel posters of places that were a roll-call of antiquity: Corinth, Syracuse, Olympus, Sparta, Delphi. But the one I liked the most was a dramatic temple fragment high on a point of land overlooking the sea. "Sounion," the poster said. "Re-Live the Story." The Greek woman who operated the BX travel booth told me, "Just take the highway south from the base. It follows the coast and takes you to Sounion in about an hour. When you get there, you'll see it. You can't go any further unless you fly off over the sea!"

I checked out an official car from the motor pool and waited at Air Ops. Deb got off the DC-3 wearing a large pack and carrying a suitcase.

"Hey, Stevie!" she said. I kissed her, put her stuff in the car, and we drove off the base to my house, where I changed into jeans and she stashed her bags. I was psyched. Now I get to show *her* some of

Greece. We munched salty black olives and chalky white feta as we drove past the southern fringes of Athens and headed down the coast. There was very little traffic, because by August, the travel gal told me, most Greeks who could afford to travel had already taken ferries to favorite islands around the Aegean or ancestral villages farther inside the mainland.

"Looks like I'm lucky," I told Deborah. "The guys who run my squadron seem fairly decent. No nut cases or Cold Warriors that I can tell." I asked about her family.

"You made a great impression," she said. "Especially with mom and David. Dom, too. He respects you for starting grad school and for being Jimmy's friend. He's hardly ever met Jimmy's friends. Or mine, either." She said her plane to Paris that night was the last flight of the evening. We had until eight in the evening to get her to the airport.

"What's this place we're going to?" she asked.

"It's magic-looking. It's a temple at the top of a point that sticks out into the sea. It's where Theseus left to go fight the minotaur at Knossos."

"How perfect," she said. "We were just there, at Knossos. What genius planning! Oh, and I've brought my usual special stuff from Turkey. Let's stop somewhere and get ready for the gods!"

We parked at the first pullout we came to overlooking the sea. We were about halfway to Sounion, according to the tourist map. The land was climbing; we were now about a hundred feet above the water. We opened the doors to let in the sea air and looked out over the fantastic seascape. Deb got out her little carved marble pipe and we smoked a piece of chocolate-brown hash the size of an aspirin. Our verbal abilities slowed as our blazing smiles stretched our faces taught in the west wind blowing off the sea. Twice I started a sentence that I couldn't finish. "The…uh…" was all that came out.

"It's just so gorgeous," I managed to say. "No matter how this place gave birth to Western civilization. Let's get going."

As we drove, we batted the two little words we fumbled over back and forth like badminton shuttlecocks. The "the" and the "and." "The…uh…" I'd start.

"Stephen," she'd answer, "Tell me about the and."

"Which first? The 'the' or the 'and'?" I'd reply. We English majors thought this was so funny and creative, we laughed our heads off. We relished the word play on this last day together, the last for an unknown length of time.

We passed several tiny fishing villages as we got to the end of the peninsula. Now three hundred feet above the sea, we parked the car at the tip of the headland. The Sounion temple to Apollo loomed before us, an exquisite white-marble fragment of a lost whole. Two lines of columns stood left to right, almost, but not quite, connected by a line of columns joining them on the eastern side. We approached the temple and stood looking up. Five slender columns, about twenty feet tall, stood in the row nearest us, and nine on the side facing the sea. On the left, only two columns remained on the east end, and none on the west end. These surviving ribs invited our minds' eyes to fill in what was missing.

Deb took my hand and we climbed onto the floor of the temple. We walked diagonally across the smooth marble blocks and stared out at the sea, at the silhouettes of islands fading in blue haze into the West. This was the last outpost of Athens civilization sailors would see as they sailed off to the wars. We lay on our backs at the southwestern corner of the temple to look up at the white columns and the sky above. When we extended our heads over the edge of the floor, we were looking upside down at the clouds and sea. Were the fleecy clouds the earth, and was the sky now the sea? White gulls slalomed in the sky, or were they gliding through the sea like penguins? We were deep into what the Greeks called the spell of sacred places, *hiera*, the presence of the gods. Undoubtedly, our flipped perception was enhanced by the hashish.

"Hello," said a voice. "Hello, please get up." A person was standing at our feet like a tall column. "You *must* get up now. Some police are coming. I will talk to you about the temple." We got up fast, our heads spinning. "I will be your guide. Walk with me and look where I point." We straightened our clothes and saw two policemen walking up onto the outer temple platform. Our guide had on gray slacks and a blue shirt under a gray cable-knit vest. Long sideburns with flecks of gray framed his dark, handsome face. He spoke good English, with a throaty accent.

"You see," he said, pointing at the view over the sea, "the king of Athens, Aegeus, waited at this high point for his son Theseus to return from trying to free Athens from their rulers in Crete by killing the Minotaur. The king had told Theseus, 'hoist a white sail that I can see from here if you come back victorious.' But Theseus forgot, or some say his white sail was torn in a storm. He did kill the Minotaur and made his way back from the labyrinth, which meant Athens had broken the hold of the Minoans upon them. But he sailed up to Sounion using his black sail. Theseus stood in the bow, hoping to see his father high above at the temple, but as the ship approached, Aegeus was so overcome with grief at not seeing the white sail that he threw himself over the edge into the sea. We call it the Aegean Sea to this day."

He took me by the elbow, turned us around, and led us to the east side of the temple. He squatted down and pointed at the myriad carvings of people's names in the blocks of marble near the bottom of a column. "You see the signature of Lord Byron? He visited here in

1810. Later he returned, hoping to raise a navy and help the Greeks gain independence from the Turks and their Ottoman Empire. But he died of a fever before he could do it." It wasn't hard to play the parts of awed tourists. Our mouths were hanging open as we made out the ornate printing of "Byron."

"Ah," our guide said, expelling a long breath. "I see our police are leaving." They were taking off their flared-up police hats as they ducked their heads getting into their car.

"I hope I didn't scare you," our guide went on. "I recognized you were in a delicate condition, and it would have been bad if the police had come upon you. They are not sympathetic."

"No, no, we thank you," I said. I was still light-headed.

"Are you really a tour guide?" asked Deb.

"No, I'm just a Greek guy," he said, smiling for the first time. "I live in Athens. I come here often."

"I'm Steve," I said, holding out my hand. "I'm here with the Air Force. This is my fiancée, Deborah."

"Call me Ari," he said. "I'm very happy to help visitors avoid problems with our police. These are tense days in our country. You must take what you experienced today as a warning you remember every day. Be well." Ari turned and went to his car, we to ours. I pulled onto the highway heading back to Athens.

I said as we pulled out, "Jesus, Deb, that was a close one!"

"As soon as we can, let's pull over," she said. "I'll throw away the hash pipe and stuff. I can't get stranded here. I've got to make that plane to Paris."

"And I don't need to start my job in Athens with a drug incident. What kind of name do you think Ari is?"

"Aristotélous, I'd bet. Aristotle," she said.

"So we got saved from the Minotaur Police by Aristotle?" We

laughed, and coughed through hash-irritated throats. We ate dinner at a roadside stand at the edge of Athens — chicken kabobs with cucumber slices and feta cheese — and I got Deb back to the base pretty close to her plane's departure time at the adjoining Athens Airport. I walked over to the terminal with her. She turned to me and looked into my eyes. Her brow and mouth conveyed sadness and regret. I moved close and embraced her. She hugged me tentatively, her straight nose hitting me in the sternum.

"Have a great time in Paris, Deb," I said. I felt proud of her and a bit jealous too. I was still stung that I had come all this way and after two days together she was leaving. She looked up at me.

"You have a great time exploring Athens. I'll think of you and I'll write," she said, her hands on my chest. "It's been so good to see you, man. You know I'll be back." We kissed each others' lips quickly, self-consciously. She turned and hustled off, leaning forward and to one side with the weight of her backpack and suitcase. At the glass door to the airport, she turned and waved. I blew her a kiss and turned toward the base, feeling a hollowness inside. *I'll just have to explore Greece without her*, I thought, as I went back to my official car.

# SEVEN

August 18th, a week after Deb left, was my 24th birthday. On the 17th, Colonel Fisher, Major Smalls and Captain Citron took me out to dinner at the Officers' Club, because the 18th fell on Sunday. I was touched that they did this for me. We went in nice civilian clothes, ordered steaks and baked potatoes and bottles of wine. They knew Deb was gone. They wanted to get to know me, which made me cautious. *Go easy on the wine, buddy,* I told myself. *Be careful what you say about your time in Mississippi. Don't let the radical cats out of the bag.*

After the steaks came and they toasted me, Colonel Fisher said, "You're from Washington, D.C., Steve, is that right?"

I didn't know what my personnel file included about me, but what could I do but just chat as if there was nothing negative in my top-secret-clearance background check. I said, "Yes, sir, born there, both parents from D.C. families, but we moved to Dallas when I was six and I grew up there." Bringing up Dallas to military guys always let me shift the discussion to the Dallas Cowboys, the NFL team that had risen to the top echelon of the league in the last two years.

"Yep, I was a sophomore in high school when the pro football franchise came to Dallas in 1960, and now I'm even more of a fan. Did you gentlemen see the division title game they won last year?"

We talked pro football for about fifteen minutes. That topic was always a good manly icebreaker. Even men who didn't follow pro football felt they had to know about the big names and top teams, and with my Cowboys background I was comfortable in the discussion. The wine flowed and the talk evolved from their favorite teams to their children and their college experiences. They seemed like nice, solid men.

When they asked about my college experiences, I told them about working at LBJ's station in Austin, dropping a class and being drafted, signing up for the Army and being switched to the Air Force by recruiting coordinator Leland Rucker. They drank in my story with amazement.

"The Air Force to the rescue," said Colonel Fisher. "I'm glad the sergeant saved you from Vietnam. The Army's loss is our gain." Captain Citron held out his glass and they all toasted my arrival in Athens.

*Didn't touch any of the sensitive stuff,* I thought. *These men seem decent and nonthreatening.*

As the waiter cleared away our plates, Al Citron, my immediate supervisor, brought up my Officer School Distinguished Graduate award. "That is really impressive, Steve. And as Colonel Fisher tells us, you followed that up with some community service in Biloxi while you were at Keesler Base. You've got a fine record already, and we're really happy to have you on our staff."

"Right, right," said the other two men. I felt accepted and respected as far as it went, as long as they didn't know how much my politics differed from theirs.

"So did you run into any of that civil-rights violence we've read so much about?" asked Major Smalls, whose face was getting flushed from the wine.

"No," I said, "although you could feel it was a police state. There was a lot of tension. Everybody walked on eggshells about race."

Smalls asked how it was a police state, and I told them that the Klan and the police had always been on the same side, that the phones were tapped and mail was opened on anybody who seemed too friendly with black people. "I worked on adult-literacy programs with an Episcopalian pastor's son who ran Head Start centers that were integrated," I said. "There were about 15 or 20 guys from the Communications Officer school who volunteered in those things."

"Well, I'll be," said Smalls. "Huh." He seemed to struggle to comment on that fact.

Al Citron and Colonel Fisher said that it was "fine community service," and they were proud the Air Force had something to do with progress in the deep South. They insisted on paying for my dinner and I thanked them profusely.

At home that night I sat in a rocking chair on my front porch with the lights off, savoring how the ocean breeze nudged away the heat of the August day. Already I could sense the social mosaic that my time in Athens would become. *I can't just dream about temples like Sounion. I've got responsibilities and supervisors watching me.* Telling my bosses even a little about Mississippi had brought back waves of memories to me of the ten months I had spent on that beautiful and dangerous segregated coast.

The Mississippi coast was so gorgeous. I hadn't even known Mississippi had a coast. Driving east from New Orleans on Highway 90 you pass estuaries where tall white shore birds stalk the water with legs bending backward. Shearwater birds skim the surface of the water, plucking little fish into their beaks. Tall pines march down from the Mississippi woods to the shore with alligator-like plates of irides-cent bark. This coast disarmed me with its beauty. I had expected to see nooses hanging from every live-oak tree.

Mississippi's biggest race riot happened in 1965, a couple of years before I arrived at Keesler Air Base. A black physician waded into the water with his congregation to protest the tradition that the white-sand beach was for whites only. The police let the Klan goons attack the blacks. My radical buddies, whom I'd met at the base, introduced me to the white minister and black doctor who had convinced the mayors of Biloxi and Gulfport that the tourist dollars would dry up if they didn't stop the Klan's marauding. The politicians ordered the Klan to keep their violence away from the tourist areas.

* * *

In the days after my birthday, the worldwide outbreaks of freedom-loving dissent continued to dominate the news. When our officers checked the squadron teletype machines they always exclaimed about stories of upheavals. On August 20, the USSR invaded Czechoslovakia with 750,000 Warsaw Pact troops, 6,500 tanks and with 800 planes, the biggest operation in Europe since the end of World War II. The Russians didn't like the Czechs enjoying their "Prague Spring" and "Velvet Revolution" under Alexander Dubcek.

The massive invasion was only 800 miles from Greece, right up the Adriatic shipping lanes. The Russian tanks rumbling through Prague were so much closer to our air base than to NATO headquarters, and so far from the United States. Colonel Fisher promptly left Athens to attend two all-day meetings of Air Force commanders to get brief-ings about Washington's plans for our region's response.

A week later, on August 22, clashes began between police and antiwar protesters at the Democratic National Convention in Chicago. We had followed the buildup to this clash in Chicago through alternative newspapers in Biloxi, from a Johnny Appleseed-like solo distributor who wore leather pants and got arrested in every town from New Orleans to Pensacola for delivering these "leftist rags."

At the Division Street diner in Biloxi we had read in those underground newspapers — *The Chicago Seed, Village Voice* and Austin's *The Rag* — about the huge coalition of end-the-war groups planning demonstrations for '67 and '68. It started out as The Spring Mobilization to End the War in Vietnam, drawing hundreds of thousands to a march from New York's Central Park to the United Nations Building in March 1967. Distinguished peace activists like David Dellinger, Father Louis Berrigan of Boston, Martin Luther King Jr. and Dr. Benjamin Spock spoke at that rally. Then 35,000 people marched from the Lincoln Memorial to the Pentagon, including writer Norman Mailer, who memorialized the surreal event by having his alter-ego, Aquarius, describe being arrested along with 650 others. The celebrated Beat poet Allen Ginsberg joined "Yippie" leaders Abbie Hoffman and Jerry Rubin in chanting on the steps of the Pentagon that they said would "levitate and exorcise" the building. I thought the defiance of these protest leaders was bold, creative and funny, a necessary and moral protest considering how the nation had been goose-stepping into this war in Asia for seven years. The "Yippie" wing of the protesters was hilarious. It was political theater by Robin Hood, Ken Kesey, Lenny Bruce and the Merry Pranksters. I was quietly pulling for them as I went about my office duties.

Captain Citron pulled up a chair by my desk and asked me if I approved of Hoffman and Rubin and the media's portraits of the rag-tag Yippies who threatened to put LSD in the Chicago water system, in addition to levitating and exorcising the Pentagon. Captain Al was curious, but I was careful.

"I bet you're glad you're not serving near Chicago, right? Sounds pretty messy. So…do you think that kind of anarchism is helpful, Steve-o?" he asked me.

"I don't think they're 'anarchists,' Al, in the old sense of anything goes. They're doing mass demonstrations, like blacks did, with a touch of put-on. They love teasing the straight world with satire." I smiled and looked him in the eyes. "Levitating the Pentagon? *Exorcising* it? That's a joke. They're doing it to get the right-wingers riled up and get press attention to their protests. But the mass demonstrations and the police reactions to them are pretty much the same as the Selma March and Memphis march by black garbage men."

"Well, that's right, the blacks did go through that too," Al said. "That was a good tactic for them. But…the civil rights people had religion on their side. They did their marches with such dignity. They didn't make jokes and threats, don't you think? They had morality on their side, didn't they?"

I was impressed that Al Citron was even discussing this with me. I swiveled my chair and faced him, enjoying this thoughtful dialogue.

"You're right about religion, Al. But there are lots of clergy in this antiwar movement. There's the Yale chaplain, William Sloane Coffin. There's Daniel Berrigan. There are the Quakers, the Catholic Workers Movement."

"Hmm," said Al. "I don't read much about that religious aspect."

"We know King was blaming the war for taking money from LBJ's anti-poverty programs," I said. "And LBJ's decision not to run — that says a lot about how he figured the whole country felt about the war."

"I guess what bothers me, Steve," said Al, "is why middle-class kids have to get so wild, with that hair and headbands and beards. They aren't in the war. They haven't had a bad life compared to blacks!"

"But the draft, Al. It's taking everybody it can reach, even though the country doesn't support the war and LBJ quit over it." I kept reminding myself to enjoy this discussion and keep my emotions from rising. "I think we have to see how long it took blacks, marching and nonviolent demonstrating from 1955 to 1963. I think the antiwar coalitions think, with over 100,000 dead in Vietnam so far and no end in sight, we can't wait eight more years like the civil rights movement had to."

Al fell silent. "Well," he said as he leaned forward and said in a low voice, "I wouldn't say this war looks like a good war with good leadership. Let's get some coffee and discuss this some more, Steve, after you get back from your remote det tour."

"Sure," I said, and we shook hands. I turned back to my desk, thinking, *I can talk to Al, but it won't be easy tiptoeing around the colonel and the major. It's like acting in a movie. But this is the price of getting here to Athens: the Air Force is paying my way.*

We continued to read the teletype stories coming in fast and furious. Between the 22nd and 28th, the Chicago police brutally put down all demonstrations, beating not only demonstrators but convention delegates, young people, old people, and news reporters indiscriminately. Network TV cameras captured riot police swinging billy clubs, trampling the crowds outside the main hotel. Chicago's Democratic machine mayor, Richard Daley, added some unintentional irony and set himself up for cutting satire when he held a news conference and announced, "The police are not here to create disorder. They're here to *preserve disorder.*"

"I knew it wasn't going to be pretty," Colonel Fisher told me. "Those police look like they were trained in Russia."

At least there was some comic relief: The Yippies nominated Pigasus, an actual pig, for president. It was obviously an insult aimed at the police, called "the pigs" in those days by minorities and the counterculture. But Pigasus was also a pun on the name of the mythical Greek flying horse, Pegasus. Even Colonel Fisher had to grin at that one. "So who are the Yippies?" he asked me.

"They say it's an acronym for Youth International Party," I said. "But I think they just love the play on 'hippies'. There's no political party involved. They're a put-on group. I think they're doing some street-theater techniques to provoke a response."

Then on August 24, France exploded its first hydrogen bomb. Those hyper-glowing balls of billowing fire and radioactivity rising into the stratosphere were the ultimate ominous sign. To those of us on the liberal side, the world was stuck under the penumbra of a Cold War eclipse that wouldn't go away.

# EIGHT

Captain Al told me, "Pack a jacket or sweater, buddy, you're going to Salonika first, and it's cool in the nighttime up there. We've assigned Trace Jackson as your driver. He's an airman first class and our most reliable courier whenever we need things delivered by hand anywhere in the country. He's up for staff sergeant already — pretty good for a guy in his late 20s. But he's had a couple of... let's just say some marital or romance issues that need to be straightened out. Nothing to affect your assignment. He's an ace driver. Not a single ticket or accident. He's a social guy, really funny one on one. You'll enjoy him."

Then Al dropped a casual but, as it turned out, life-changing assignment on me. "Before you leave, I need you to go to a transportation meeting for me. Did you know you're the new squadron transportation officer?"

"No, I didn't," I said.

"Well, now you know. You're the logical one. Not that logic interrupts what we do here all that much. I'm glad to pass it on to you. It's a good way for you to meet some important people. Tomorrow morning, you and Trace will hit the road for Salonika."

*A transportation meeting? Exactly the boring stuff I thought would start after I got back from touring the country. Bummer!* I took a base motor-pool car because the Officers' Club was over in Glyfada, about a mile from the base. I parked the dark blue Chevy two-door at a curb about two blocks from the club.

"Blueyob!" I heard someone call out.

I finished locking the car and turned to walk down the sidewalk.

"Blue yob!" There it was again. Blue what? The car? The voice came from a woman driving a white Fiat that had eased up by the curb and was tracking me as I walked. She was leaning over, gesturing to me from the passenger window. I walked over to the window and said "What?" I figured she wanted directions.

"*Blue yob!!*" I was drawing a blank. Blue was the Air Force color and the Greek national color. I stared at this woman, tongue-tied. She made a face of exasperation, reached into her blouse, and pulled a bare breast into view with her palm. "Blueyob!" she insisted, pointing to her lap with the other hand. Ooooh! *Blow job!* I hesitated a second — was I on Candid Camera or being set up by base security? No; there didn't appear to be anyone else within a block in either direction.

The second I realized that she was a prostitute, I also realized that as a 24-year-old virgin I needed to learn some things about sex. It seemed the cleanest and simplest way, since she wasn't inviting me into a hotel room where I could be photographed or trapped. If we stayed in her car, this was as close to quick and anonymous as liaisons got. So I got in.

"Okay," she said, straightening her shirt, her eyebrows knit together in disbelief. She seemed about forty, with shoulder-length ash-blond hair pulled back behind her ears. She was wearing a short, tight skirt and a loose beige blouse that now had the top three buttons unbuttoned. She put the Fiat in gear, zoomed around the corner and pulled over halfway down the block. A second thought dawned on me: *I'm on duty, performing official base business. Could be a legal violation. But look at this deserted street. There's nobody around.*

She was an expert — efficient and gentle. A flood of deep relief came over me, opening the door on my adult sex life. I cradled her head in both hands for a moment, exhaling deeply and loving that she'd taken me across this threshold. She took my hands in hers and gently removed them from her head, gave me some tissues, opened the door, spit into the street, wiped her mouth with some more tissues, put the Fiat in gear and zoomed back around the block to where she'd picked me up.

"Endaxi?" she said with a smile, Greek for OK? She told me the price, about five bucks U.S., and shooed me out.

"Zee you again?"

"Endaxi," I said. I got back into my car and sat there, enjoying the endorphins. My heart beat in a deep bass drum note. A curb-service encounter with a woman I didn't know in the anonymity of a street in an Athens suburb. She materialized and disappeared in a flash. So I was no longer a virgin. Or partially not. I didn't feel guilty. I didn't feel dirty. I felt happy that I'd taken the offer and learned something.

I started my car, then remembered: *Wait! The meeting at the officers' club! So, that must be the Glyfada Gobbler!* I checked my uniform for stains and got out of the car. *Oh yeah, Colonel, I'll be sure to avoid her. Right! And Al, you did say I'd meet some important people. That happened.*

The meeting about Air Force transportation rules and proce-dures was boring, naturally. They didn't mention the transportation rule I'd just broken with the Gobbler, about using base vehicles for illegal purposes. Whatever they did cover made little impression on my brain, soaked as it was in the chemicals just recently released in a white Fiat. I went up to the chairman of the meeting, introduced myself, and asked for a copy of the agenda. He understood that my notes might need some fortifying, my being brand new at the base, and all.

I went into the bar and sat on a stool beside two flamboyantly drunk fly-boys, pilots with their soft folded cloth caps scrunched illegally down on their heads, top-gun style. I said hello, but they just nodded.

"By God, I know one thing," said the one closest to me, twirling his beer bottle and peeling at the label with his thumbnail. He was still talking to his friend. "Come in from the east an' you shoot right over the fuckin' runway."

"Well I'll tell you one goddamn thing," said the other, who was staring at a group of Greek young ladies walking up the sidewalk to the O club. Neither finished their sentences. These were not real top guns, I hoped. Or the pilots of the hop to Crete and back, either. That was a short and routine flight, but I didn't think it would help to have hungover pilots. I finished my beer and walked out. I wasn't thinking of Deborah quite as much, and I walked to my car with a loose lilt.

The next morning Trace Jackson and I embarked on my tour of Greece. As we drove north out of Athens, the yellowish-brown layer of pollution extended out from the city till it hit surrounding mountain ranges, which helped keep it in. The roads were crowded with cars and their wild drivers until we got an hour outside Athens and its northern suburbs. With the sky clear and most of the traffic gone, I got my first look at the inland landscape away from the coasts. The mountains stunned me. They weren't nearly as high as the Rockies, but they went up steeply from sea level. Beautiful groves of trees hugged the contours of the land.

"What are these trees?" I asked.

"The gray-green ones are olive trees. The tall dark pointy ones are some kind of cypress. You know what? Why don't you call me Trace? Everybody does."

"Okay," I said. Clumps of dark cypress spires punctuated the rolling olive groves. It was a landscape that had been sculpted for centuries for its beauty. Stone walls ran up hills and down swales. Little whitewashed stucco chapels sat at intersections of footpaths. Ancient-looking villages; herds of sheep and goats walking down the road with bells clinking, a shepherd holding a long stick; grapevines and fruit trees planted in rows and tucked onto terraces; people in the fields whose loose clothing and lined faces made me think of the Middle Ages. If it weren't for the occasional cars, we might have been traveling through a Van Gogh landscape in France.

Trace was a smart, handsome black guy with gleaming, long, straightened hair and a great smile — a major ladies' man. It was impossible for us to maintain the officer-enlisted wall of formality. "Did you see those Scandinavian girls, Lieutenant?" he'd say as we passed through a village where a little group of tall young ladies, all with long blond hair, stood outside a taverna talking. He lowered his dark glasses to make big eyes at me. "That blonde hair stands out, huh? Shall we circle back and see if they need a ride?"

"So, are they tourists?"

"Oh yeah. You never see that many tall blond Greeks! Swedish and Danish gals come down here to get some sun. They're pretty open about sex, too."

I found out later that Trace had impregnated three other airmen's wives in a three-month period, so they sent him to a hospital in Germany on sick leave so the squadron could cool down over it and the chaplains could decide what to do. Military folks generally scorned "free love" and the new fashion of hippie chicks going braless, but at the military bases I saw in 1969, it looked like there was a *ton* of sleeping around.

Trace not only showed me the way to Thessaloniki, he taught me my first lessons in how to act in tavernas, bars and village streets. We pulled into several roadside tavernas on the long ride to Thessaloniki. "Look around for the parents or owners before you flirt with the waitress," he said. "If she's alone, you got a great chance of scorin'. They love Americans. I mean the people, y'know, not the government. In bars, go off to a little table and scope the joint out. Don't stand at the bar; you'll have to accept some guy's offer to buy you a drink. If you do, it's everybody else's sacred honor to buy you one too, and 'less you got a stomach and liver like iron, they'll drink you under the bar. You don't want the police or base security havin' to come and pick your ass up." He cackled with glee. "'Scuse my French, Sir."

"If I'm gonna call you Trace, you have to call me Steve."

"Okay Steve, fair is fair."

It took all day to drive north to Salonika, as Colonel Bert had called it, across some beautiful country. My tourist guide map showed that the Greeks called Salonika Thessaloníki. Aha! It was the city that the Apostle Paul wrote his first and second letters to the "Thessalonians," two books in the Christian Bible. The scholars say they were the first New Testament books written. I read Trace some lines from my guidebook: "Get this: Paul either wrote it from Athens, or, possibly, from Corinth, in 52 AD. He must have been down there writing Corinthians, too. He's encouraging the new Christians to give up all their pagan ways."

"Yeah, Lieutenant, whoops, I mean Steve, there's all kindsa levels to this place," said Trace. "Old Paul traveled this exact way we are. And to Corinth, too, right? Which is where we'll go after we leave here. It's a trip, huh? I was raised Christian, so my mama loves to hear where I been over here. I tell her, 'Turn your Bible to Thessalonians, or Corinthians, and imagine me right there.' She's in Chicago, South Side, with my two little brothers." He pushed his weight back into the seat, sighed, and moved his toothpick to the other side of his mouth. "Course I don't tell her about the young ladies. Or the commies. Or the contraband you can buy. You know?"

The universe had assigned me another great guide.

We drove through the outskirts of Thessaloniki at sunset. Greece's second largest city, it was a jumble of buildings that looked like they'd come from every century and religion. It still had its white Byzantine defensive walls in places, and a church modeled on Haghia Sophia, the great mosque in Istanbul. Trace pointed out a huge ruined arch made for Roman Emperor Constantine. As we drove into the city, I saw guys in the streets wearing antique folk clothes: wool knee pants or balloon-style pants gathered at the ankle like in old illustrations from the Middle East. I saw black eyes, green eyes, blue eyes, handlebar mustaches and embroidered brimless caps. This was the remote Balkan Greek culture that blended into Muslim Albania and Bulgaria. Now we were in a different *National Geographic* article. Athens seemed like New York City compared to this.

Trace said, "Don't know whether the communist thing or the Muslim thing takes longer to figure out." We were getting into the center of the city. "Coulda made it here in four hours if we had to," said Trace, "but I wanted you to see the countryside. Great, innit? Now this hotel is where we're staying." He pulled up to a two-story building on the corner of a square filled with tilting market stalls and sidewalk vendors selling cheese, goat meat, dates and cigarettes. I asked him why we didn't just go to the site, and he said that there was a routine to follow since it was so close to the communist border.

"We get to go out to eat here tonight, then you go to the det tomorrow morning. They'll send a car to getcha. Let's unload, take a shower, then go eat."

Trace and I changed into jeans. He took me to a restaurant, where we ate steaks and fries and drank Fix, the national brand of Greek beer. "See, Lieutenant? The fix is in!" Trace grinned and raised his eyebrows twice. We talked about our childhoods. His mom was a teacher like mine. He and his dad didn't see eye to eye, like me and mine. He was thinking of coming back to Europe after he got out of the Air Force, "'Cause it's easier to be black here."

I asked him how.

"Well, it's not like people are angels over here. They may still have some racism. But lots of them are curious about black people.

They don't just automatically think you're a bum or a crook like lots of Americans do."

On our second Fix, we talked about sports. He was a great fan of the Chicago Bears and the Cubs baseball team. I knew a bit about those teams and their heroes: Dick Butkus, the insanely aggressive Lithuanian middle linebacker, and Ernie Banks, the black shortstop known as "Mr. Cub."

I was really happy about my first day with Trace. We had talked about bars, women, the Greek landscape, the New Testament, and sports in his town and my town. Trace Jackson had become more of a friend to me than anybody in mainland Greece so far. I thought back to the day I had to decide whether to accept the military draft or escape it. A day like this, spent driving through the beauty and history and lore of Greece with a great companion, like the days with Deborah on Knossos and Sounion, made my decision feel like exactly the right one.

Walking back to the hotel in the dark around ten o'clock, Trace instructed me to walk in the middle of the sidewalk, "case any trouble comes from a doorway or a car, you got room to move. And don't look anybody in the eyes." My pulse ticked up a notch. *Is he kidding me?* "Aww, don't sweat it," he said, noticing my apprehension. "But we do have to know how to be careful, and ready for anything."

Back at the hotel, fiddling with the tiny TV until we picked up a dubbed version of "Gunsmoke," I asked Trace for some background on the city's recent reputation. He told me Thessaloniki has been a hot spot for left-wing demonstrations for at least four years. He singled out a local delegate to the Parliament in Athens, named Lambrakis.

"The cops killed him back in '64. Ever since then, whenever the students want to protest these colonels running the government, kids from the Lambrakis clubs lead the demos. That's why we don't wear uniforms around here at night. Not that it's too hard to see we're Ammies anyway."

"Ammies?"

"That's the nickname for us. The Americans. The old people call us 'A-mer-íchi,' or something like that. I used to think they thought I was Alan Ameche, the pro football guy."

I thought about Deborah, walking the streets of another great city with angry students in the streets. *I wish she could be here with us. This is like a tour with an insider, and she'd like Trace. I wonder how she's doing. I hope she writes soon. I miss her.*

Trace went downstairs and came back with some brandy, which escorted us to dreamland. We slept well on the creaky bedsprings and thin mattresses of the two twin beds. It was cold that night. We were perched above an arm of the Aegean Sea, and wind came off the harbor. At seven-thirty we went down to the café off the small lobby for breakfast, cigarette smoke already floating in the room, and had little cups of Turkish coffee, croissants and cheese, and scrambled eggs. Two Ammies dressed in jeans came in the front door and joined us. They introduced themselves as the det couriers here to pick me up. They showed me their Comm Squadron IDs and we got up to leave.

"I'll see you tomorrow right back here, Lieutenant," said Trace. "Give my regards to the guys."

The detachment's courier vehicle was a battered Fiat.

"This is a squadron vehicle?" I asked the guys as we drove north out of the city.

"Sure is, Lieutenant. Looks funky, but underneath the hood there's a Sunbeam Alpine straight six, bored out and stroked. If we get in a tight spot, this tub can flat move. We're not far from the Macedonian border and the Bulgarian border. It's the Red Boonies up here, Sir."

I imagined Bulgarians living in log huts with their goats and chickens, wearing wooden shoes and fezzes. I looked out the window to hide my smile at the thought that two days ago I was sitting in a suburb with a sweet woman's head bobbing in my lap, and a few days before that Deb and I were frolicking around a palace ruin on Crete. *Wow! What a tour!*

This was a small country, the mainland not quite 200 miles long, the population not quite seven million. Yet each island and each province seemed its own world.

Our radio relay detachment was Spartan — isolated and austere. I pitied the guys assigned there and, in my report, recommended a new darkroom enlarger, resupply of film development chemicals, and replacements for their cards, dominoes, checkers, Monopoly and all the other board games they'd worn out in their boredom.

\* \* \*

The next day, after meeting Trace according to plan, he drove us toward Corinth. The landscape continued to be mountainous and rugged, like Colorado in places, interspersed with olive trees and cypress sentinels. The sunny sides of hills glowed with the gold, white and red of wildflowers.

We stopped at a taverna and sipped Fixes and ate olives and cheese and Ritz crackers in little cellophane packages. Some local young ladies came in to buy Cokes and candy. They eyed us, and Trace flirted with them. When they left, I said, "You're a flirtin' fool, Trace."

He grinned. "Oh, well, I do love the girls."

"Ever met any you didn't like?"

"Well, you got to be careful of some of the Greek gals who just want to be with an Ammie to get your money and maybe a trip to the States. Guys have told me that some Greek gals use Ammies to lose their virginity too, somebody the family and village will never know. Same with Scandinavian girls down here on summer trips, they use the Greek guys, and visa-versa. And some of the wives of the airmen at the base, they're bored, or they're frustrated. Or some never thought they'd be around a black guy and wanna check me out. When they're offerin', I'm not gonna turn it down, Steve, know what I mean?"

"You said married gals?"

He took a swig and looked out at the hills around this little village. "Well, you'll find out that there're a lot of unhappy people at this base. At every base I've been to. There's people on pills — Valium, Librium — they don't know what they're doing. And of course everybody drinks. I love sleeping with women. Maybe I don't know what I'm doin' either. Least I don't do pills and wake up at the wrong house."

"Sounds like "As the World Turns" meets the Age of Aquarius, huh?" I said.

"Oh yeah, man: harmony and understanding," he smiled back.

"And even in backwards ol' Greece, too."

"Sympathy and trust abounding, Steve. Hee, hee."

I smiled at our back-and-forth irony. But when I thought of Trace's insight about the many unhappy people at the base, I asked for his opinion about why that was.

"The base is a real small world. Some people can be cool with that, mostly the real religious or the ones with little kids. They build their lives around the church groups or the ball field or basketball gym. I think that works for some, but really, most of 'em don't get out from the base to know the Greeks and the culture, or whatever country they're in, and they get bored or depressed with the little world behind the fence."

I thought of The Gobbler. *What a desperate and boring living she made. Our men going to Greek prostitutes is the lowest common denominator of our two countries' unequal fit. I wonder if she, or any of them, is really as cheerful and self-supporting as Ilya, the Greek prostitute played by Melina Mercouri, in* Never on Sunday, *the film that introduced a lot of Greek culture to the world and won Oscars a few years ago. I don't think so.*

# NINE

The day after leaving Thessaloniki, we drove into Corinth, about 50 miles west of Athens, where we found the most spectacular old acropolis in all of Greece. It was perched on top of a stone monolith that soared nearly 2,000 feet above the narrow isthmus that connected Greece to its huge southern peninsula, called the Peloponnesus. The isthmus neck of land itself stood hundreds of feet above the two seas it divided, the Saronic Gulf to the east, an arm of the Aegean Sea, and the Gulf of Corinth to the west, an arm of the Adriatic, looking toward Italy.

We decided to climb up to the old acropolis and asked in the modern town sprawling below it.

"Oh, you will need *great tennis shoes*!" said a man at the town museum. "It will take you four, five hours to go up and back. And there are no more prostitutes up there to soothe you. Ha ha ha!"

He said that in the old days the temple at the top was devoted to Aphrodite, and there were 2,000 sacred prostitutes, most above but some down in the town, to entertain all the pilgrims. As we didn't have *great tennis shoes*, we turned away; but he said, "Or, you can take a taxi!"

This tour of the remote detachments was turning out to be even cooler than I had expected. It was like finding Yellowstone National Park a short drive from Yosemite. At the top of the acropolis, called Acrocorinth, a strong fresh sea wind blew between the two gulfs. The views were spectacular—you could almost see Athens to the east and, to the south, how the Peloponnese, which was half the land area of Greece, spread from this tiny land bridge. Trace bought postcards that mentioned Paul having written the Corinthians here.

"Nope, I ain't sendin' Mom one that mentions the prostitutes!" The brochures in the tourist office told us that Paul had written to the Corinthians to get them to give up their carnal ways. Trace and I laughed about the oxymoron, in our modern world, of "sacred prostitutes" and how that might have worked.

*The Gobbler, I thought. Related to Aphrodite? And me, another pilgrim.*

* * *

Back in Athens, I found a notice on the base bulletin board for Greek lessons and called the number. It turned out to be a half-Greek, half-British woman named Jean, who was a licensed guide at Corinth, Delphi and all the other archaeological sites. I told her my name and asked to meet her.

"Certainly, Stephanie," she answered, and gave me directions.

"Stephanie?" I said. "Isn't that the female version of Stephen?"

"It's with an -e, not an -ie," she said. "We call you Stephanos when talking about you, and Stephané when talking to you," she said.

I went to her family's apartment. She was short, spoke upper-class British English, had brown hair swept up into a ducktail, brown eyes with lavender eye-shadow, and was cute and energetic. Her

mother was polite but grave and suspicious, but Jean and I hit it off
and decided to meet once a week for language lessons. I told Trace
about her.

"Turns out we just missed her at Corinth last week," I said. "She
speaks British English and is kind of cute."

Trace gave me a look and a grin.

"Nah," I said, "not my type."

"What is your type?"

"Oh," I said, thinking of Deborah, "somebody funny and satirical.
Somebody we'd call hip."

"Oh, a hippie chick!" laughed Trace.

"No, not a hippie, somebody who, you know, knows what's
going on."

"I was just ribbin' ya," Trace said. "I knew what you meant. A
government guide doesn't seem like you at all."

I met with her a few days later at a tiny table in the living room of
her parents' apartment. Her father had been British Consul in Athens,
and her mother was Greek. Jean became my language teacher and first
Greek oracle. As I thought, she was very conservative, but she taught
me some classical Greek, some street Greek, and lots of myths and
history. Our studying turned animated and we leaned closer, looking
at pictures in books and at her handwritten word lessons. She loved
words, knew several languages, and could gossip about the Greek
gods and goddesses as if they were her relatives. I began to feel tingles
at the back of my neck listening to her. And then her fragrance drifted
into my nostrils. Then we touched! I had tingles all over me now. We
were doomed.

It started innocently enough. On our third lesson, Jean realized
that I needed some basic tutoring in how to write Greek in its Cyrillic
alphabet. The capitals were hard enough: D was a triangle; S was an

E; A had no crossbar; small i was an n with a tail; theta and pi weren't math symbols, they were letters. And when Jean wrote in Cyrillic cursive, the letters lost even the slight familiarity of algebra characters. Her cursive version of "Stephanos" might as well have been written in hieroglyphics.

She would write a Greek word, then print it and swivel the page ninety degrees so I could read it, tilting my head toward her, her head tilted toward me, holding her finger at the "upsilon" or "ypsilon," and my hand, tracing the letters, came softly into contact with hers; we went on to the next vowel or consonant giving me trouble, delta or gamma or kappa, and our knees and fingers began to touch as we pored over our lessons.

Her mother spied on us, sneaking quietly into the kitchen from a back room. Jean told me later that her mother had said, "Him, the American, I don't see him well." She felt the vibes and smelled the pheromones all the way in the back room. Her daughter was engaged to a proper older Greek man but was now sitting at the tiny table with this Ammie. On the fourth lesson I brought her Leonard Cohen's *Spice-Box of Earth*. The cover of the paperback was an open box covered with designs, including a tasteful nude woman on one side.

We looked into each other's eyes and agreed that it would be a good change of pace to meet the next time at the Athens Hilton, for a late-evening recap of our progress so far. Two days later, we sat in a dark corner in the Delphine bar and couldn't keep our hands off each other under the table.

"You leave first, Stephané," she said. "Wait in the alley. I'll follow in five minutes." I left money for the bill on the table and went out a back door, the location of which she drew for me on her napkin. In the twilight, I saw her shut the hotel door behind her and come down the loading-dock steps. We swept into an embrace in the dark, her purse falling to the pavement, our mouths fusing together, our hands caressing.

Jean and I canceled the language lessons at her family's apartment and began meeting in her car on Athens streets at night or on remote suburban streets during the day. The physical attraction had hit us like a squall in the gulf. After Deborah and the Gobbler, Jean was totally fifties, with her cashmere sweaters and scarves around her neck and stockings and ... a *girdle*. The second time, parked on a quiet street, we almost went horizontal in the front seats, dodging the shift lever. It was an odd throwback to parking and necking with high-school girlfriends in my mother's car back in Dallas, fearing discovery and rushing intimacy in the awkward spaces of a car. But this was in Athens with an engaged woman who, I thought, certainly must know what she was doing.

I had never tried going to third base with somebody wearing a girdle. It was thick and tight, an effective barrier, and my hand almost went numb under the layers of elastic. It was a contraceptive garment. The fact that she didn't help me or use her superb English brought things to a standstill. She said she had to leave, anyway. The next time I saw her, I asked her to go to a movie downtown, and she said she couldn't be seen with me in public because of her arranged marriage.

"I've been engaged to Yorgos for three years. I don't want a scandal, I want to keep leading tours."

"So where is this going?" I asked.

"It doesn't mean we can't see each other. We can meet at various places. But no one must know."

"So what if your fiancé caught us?"

"We'll make sure he won't," she said. "You Americans ... you're so puritanical! Greeks understand this. My parents arranged the marriage. And I like you." She laughed at my innocence.

*Me, puritanical?* I thought. *If she only knew about Deborah on Knossos or the Glyfada Gobbler.* Then a sobering thought hit me: *Was I Jean's gobbler?*

The truth was, I didn't really *like* Jean. I turned toward her and said, "I don't want to have to sneak around to see you, Jean. I don't want to have an engaged lover." Another sobering thought came: *according to the Air Force, I'm engaged too.* We were parked behind the archaeological museum where many of Jean's tours started, on Bouboulinas Street.

"I'm only going to be here for two years," I told her. "I don't want to spend what time I've got this way."

"But why only two years? Can't you have a career with your military here? Move up the ladder?"

"No. I'm a draftee, Jean, and I'd never extend my time in the military. As soon as my enlistment is up, in two years, I'm gone."

She sighed. Looked at me. Looked out the window. "What *do* you want then, Stephané?" she asked. I looked away. Even though I thought I'd already told her, that wasn't easy to answer. None of the girls I'd dated had ever asked me that. I'd never asked a girlfriend that, or asked myself what I wanted in a girl, either.

Faint bouzouki music drifted to us from the radio of a passing car. A woman pushed a baby stroller and herded two toddlers across the street ahead of us. *I have an outsider spirit now, despite being in the military. Jean's a consummate insider of the upper class. Not my cup of retsina.*

"I want to be with someone who is free to be with me," I said. "I don't want to be told when and where I can see you." I thought of Deborah. She was a dissident like me and free to be with me...but she wasn't here. Suddenly, my monologue was pierced by a wailing scream from across the street. Chills ripped up my spine. I jerked my head around and looked toward the sound.

"What the hell was that?"

"Oh, it's just the police beating a suspect," said Jean offhandedly. "That's the main police station, across the street. Probably a communist." The sound of a motorcycle started up, competing with the screams.

"Doesn't this bother you?" I asked Jean. "Hearing somebody being tortured right beside the place you work?"

"Stephen. One of the many things you don't know about Greece is what a threat the communists have been to us. The Colonels aren't angels, but Athens has been peaceful since they took over. No, I don't mind screaming if it comes from a communist. I prefer it to the screaming of innocents in a burning car or building."

"But how do you know who they're beating in there? Lots of cops are thugs. You're not clairvoyant."

"I trust the police more than I do the dissidents," she said curtly. Jean had a tour lined up at the museum. She got out.

"Good-bye, then, Stephané," she said.

"Good-bye, Jean. For good." *Wow. I'm glad that happened. Don't want to spend another minute with her.* The motorcycle across the street sputtered on.

I thought about this sudden romance and sudden breakup for several days as Trace and I made the final calls on our detachments. I kept feeling like the physical part of sex, which I had thought was mysterious and difficult, turned out not to be that hard to get, compared to this emotional and mental part Jean and Deb and I had plunged into. Jean called my house once, about a month later, "just to say hello," she said. I had no interest in talking to her, nor could I figure out why she'd called me.

"How are you?" I asked. *You don't care,* I thought. *Say good-bye and hang up.*

"I'm fine, Stephané." A long pause.

"Good-bye, Jean."

I never heard from her again. Deborah remained at the top of my list. Wait — she was the only one on the list.

We made our way to the last Comm Squadron Detachment on my tour of the country, far on the western fringe of Greece, with no ruins nearby and with a tragic modern neighbor overlooking it: Jackie Kennedy Onassis. The obscure little island of Skorpios was mostly owned by Aristotle Onassis, a shipping billionaire who had a fortified villa that looked down on our little Quonset-hut detachment across a neck of water. Guys at our det said Jackie would send couriers over in motorboats to borrow movies that our Athens office sent out.

"Wow," I told Trace. "Jackie, out here in this nowhereville! You know, JFK was killed in my town, Dallas. I loved him."

"I did too," said Trace. "First guy to ever mention civil rights on TV. He and Bobby and Teddy playing football on the White House lawn was pretty cool, too."

We stood at the edge of the det and looked across the water at Skorpios island.

"It's weird, you know? I feel worse about Jackie being here, this close to Albania, for Pete's sake. It seems like total exile."

"I know," said Trace. "It's no Camelot over here, that's for damn sure."

Back at home in Athens, I found a postcard from Deb waiting in my office mailbox. "Philippe is sick but still printing for Cartier-B. I hang out at a café near St. Germain. I'm on the dean's list. Paris is cold. Write me." *Write her? Where? The address is unreadable!* I missed her so much, and I wanted her to say she missed me. I longed to get one of her multipage letters, and to send her one of mine. I hadn't been physically faithful to her, nor she to me, I imagined. That, among so many other things, would be interesting to talk about. But I was still faithful to our possibilities together, in my heart and in my mind.

In another two weeks my car arrived on a freighter from Biloxi, and I went down to the port of Piraeus to pick it up. Major Smalls said I'd had enough travel and needed to start giving the daily briefings to the colonel about the traffic on the radio channels. So nights and weekends, I began to explore Athens on my own, tooling around the old heart of the city along its narrow mazelike streets.

I came to cherish my fragrant little yard in Glyfada, with its orange blossoms and roses. The toxic air of downtown Athens was eating layers off the marble antiquities. Driving through the fumes of the traffic, I would get brief whiffs of pizza or roasting lamb or a woman's perfume, or the stench of a sewer. But all of the odors were fleeting.

Driving my own car, things sped up. I would soon find some of the social fault lines under the teeming city. I had lied my way into an assignment in Greece, had lost the girlfriend I came here to be with, got a splendid house and then they sent me on a tour of the whole country before I even punched the time clock. I felt they've gift-wrapped Greece for me, and I had better get ready for everything I was meant to learn about myself here. So far I had only learned that lust was easy and love was a mysterious journey I had no map for. With no family near and no routine ruts of home to channel my way, I felt as if I could meet an important life lesson around any corner, on any day. This was the thrill of living in a strange land.

# TEN

One day when I thought everybody had gone to lunch, I stayed at my desk and heard a song blare from our squadron's maintenance area in the back of the building that I never thought I'd hear in Athens: the joyous funk of Sly and the Family Stone:

*I want to take you high-yah! Baby baby baby light my fi-yah!*
*Boom shaka-laka-laka, Boom shaka-laka-laka…*

Soul music! As I got up, I realized it was radio, as an American DJ–style voice gabbed: "This new one from Sly goes out to the Transportation Squadron and Air Ops night shifts, you know who you are." Sly and the Family Stone projected one of the happiest, loosest, and most infectious sounds from the USA, like a bunch of people on a front porch inviting everybody to jam and dance with them. And here it was wafting through our office, maybe out over the quiet suburb of Glyfada and even over the Acropolis.

I zoomed back to maintenance, where Trace Jackson sat holding a burger and grinning.

"Hey, Trace, I didn't know anybody was here!"

"That's why I'm turnin' up the volume, Steve! They're all signed out till 1:30."

"Is that our base radio station?"

"Sure is," he said, doing a funky move to the music, still holding his hamburger out to the side, a tomato slice hanging on for dear life.

"I heard we had a station. So, where is it?" I asked.

"Right *there*! First building past the ball diamond," he said, as if everybody knew.

When I walked over to the unmarked base radio station, I introduced myself as a radio guy from Austin, Texas. The guy on the mike was Craig Barker from Utah, an airman first class with attitude.

"Sly and the Family Stone, man! That's a sound for sore ears. How far does this signal carry?" I asked.

"To the far edges of Athens, my friend. I'm in trouble for playing that one. Too funky. It wasn't on the playlist we get from the mother station in California. I also played Sly's "Stand" last night on the jazz show. Got about ten calls from Greek teenagers wanting the lyrics. I'll hear it for that one, for sure. Won't be as much trouble as we got into for Barry McGuire's 'Eve of Destruction' — 'You're old enough to kill, but not for votin'.' But hey, *that* was worth getting docked a day's pay for anyway."

Barker was suave and confident, about six-three, with shiny hair combed straight back. Right away we told each other we were Craig and Steve, as long as nobody else was around. But then he pulled out his address book to make sure I knew *he* knew famous music people. "See that? That's Bill Evans' private phone number in New York."

"Bill Evans?"

"Uh…piano? On Miles Davis's 'Kind of Blue'?"

I shrugged.

"Best-selling jazz album of all time? Best *Down Beat* trumpet player three times? Best jazz composition for 'Sketches of Spain'?"

I would've told Craig that my roommate had played Stan Kenton charts and knew all the big-band styles but saw that Craig was on a mission to top me in record knowledge.

"This is Ben Webster's," he said, holding his address book out for me to see. But — he did have a wall jammed with shelves of American music albums, which I was delighted to see, and the second most interesting person I'd met on base after Trace.

He put on "Greenfields" by the Brothers Four. "That'll cool down the Sly Stone," he said. "We have thousands of Greek listeners out there, Steve, tens of thousands. The Colonels — the *Greek* colonels — have banned American music, but they can't ban us. I can't tell you how many calls we get from Greeks: 'Play Simon and Garfunkel, Joan Baez, Johnny Cash, The Beatles, the soundtrack from *Hair*, 'Born to be Wild,' 'Chain of Fools,' 'Sittin' on the Dock of the Bay,' 'Dance to the Music.' On and on, man! We slip in a Bob Dylan or Leonard Cohen every once in a while. Boy, different people call in from the shadows, man. Then we have to go, 'Duh, Sarge, I don't know *how* that got in there.'" He swiveled around expertly, sliding played albums into their foot-square sleeves, stacking to-play albums at the ready, checking off things on his log sheet. "Our biggest Greek audience by far is for the jazz show after dark — Sinatra, Billie Holiday, Sarah Vaughn, Benny Goodman, Miles. No station *in all of Greece* plays American music."

"You're kidding," I said.

"Nope. We're it. The Greek government has flat outlawed jazz and rock 'n' roll. All of pop music — even covers by French singers, if we can call that pop." He made a gagging motion with his finger down his throat. "But the agreement that allows the base to be here stipulates that we can entertain our own people with our music! We just power up the transmitter so it goes out to the whole town. The embassy's secretly behind us. I have drinks all the time with USIS guys who slip me a list of requests. It's sneaky *propa-ganda*. The Greeks don't have the gear to jam us and wouldn't try it anyway, or we'd stop the flow of bananas and toaster ovens into Piraeus."

"What's the USIS?"

"Stands for U.S. Information Service. You don't know them? They're the 'cultural' staffers at the embassy," he said, making air quote marks. "They're the propaganda staffers."

"You hang out with them?"

"You'll meet 'em all at the big Christmas party at the embassy. I deejay for their functions. Music makes you many friends, my friend."

Barker became my confidant. We hit it off, mostly, because we both loved the music that was pouring out in those days and loved talking on the radio to the unseen thousands out there listening.

One night as Barker's jazz shift was winding down, a guy called in saying he was looking for American voices to dub a "spaghetti western," one of those films made with a cheap international cast hired for their faces, that a small studio then dubs into several languages.

Then Barker handed me the phone. That's how I met Allan Wenger. He had a smooth baritone voice with a touch of New York accent. Allan invited us to join him and some friends at Kolonaki Square that night about eleven, so we could talk about the dubbing gig. I'd heard that Kolonaki, located between the Acropolis and Lycabettus Hill, was the most trendy, happening square in Athens. It was said to be jammed with chic designer shops, cafés and people hanging out in sidewalk bars seeing and being seen. Barker said the scene just gets started at eleven, buzzing on to the wee hours.

When Craig's show ended, we drove in my VW bug past the Hilton Hotel to the edge of downtown, where two six-lane roads merged. It looked like everybody with a car was merging, honking, yelling and rubbernecking out their windows. I eased the gray VW into the tide of little sardine cars — lots of Fiat 500s, the smallest car ever mass produced. About half the cars needed a muffler job and the other half were honking. I was sure my VW was going to get T-boned. The guy ahead of me stuck his hand out at the driver in front of him, fingers spread wide.

"That's right, buddy, give him five," said Barker.

"What's that?"

"'Giving five' to Greeks is roughly like giving the finger, only you give 'all five'," said Barker. "Means the father, son, holy ghost, Mary Magdalene, and a fifth saint of your choice, I think, something like that. 'May they all curse you, asshole.' It's no surprise that Greece leads all of Europe in traffic deaths per capita. And in vehicular fights over nothing."

This was the first traffic circle, or "roundabout" as the Brits called them, I'd ever seen. We were rotating on the outer edge of this traffic whirlpool, and I missed our turnoff. I put on my signal and looked to go inward a layer, and of course the guy next to me stood on his horn and gave me five. "Fuck him," said Barker and rolled down his window to give him five over the top of the VW. This was like Big Boy bumper cars at the State Fair.

The guy looked at us with his eyes bugging out and threw *two fives* at us, letting go of the wheel and yelling some obscenity. I pressed on the brake pedal. A horn immediately blared behind me.

"Don't hit the brakes!" yelled Barker. "There's always somebody right behind you! Just let off on the gas!"

The exhaust fumes were nauseating. At least they weren't throwing tire irons or beer bottles — just five fingers. We suddenly came abreast of our exit and I veered into another major boulevard, Vasilissis Sophias street. Barker gave directions to turn here, turn there. We parked on a narrow side street the way they do in Greece, two wheels up on the sidewalk. The smell of roasting lamb and thyme wafted from a street vendor's stall. A woman wearing a black scarf was turning wooden skewers of meat over a grill on a cart. We gave her six drachs, about $1.50 US, and walked two blocks to Kolonaki Square, each holding two skewers of meat like corn on the cob and pulling the spicy lamb off with our teeth.

When we rounded a corner, the view opened onto Kolonaki Square, and my jaw dropped. "Cool, eh?" said Barker, striding into the crowd of people ringing the square, hitching up his pleated linen slacks and smoothing his hair back. Little round tables filled the sidewalks. Waiters with expressionless faces came out of the cafés at full steam,

somehow negotiating the gauntlet of knees and feet to deliver bottles of wine, mineral water and ouzo, little cups of steaming coffee, and trays of sweets. We were about halfway around the square when I saw a guy stand up and wave at us. He had thinning black hair, long sideburns and a big grin. Barker broke into his toothy smile, and we wended toward this little table. It was Allan Wenger.

"How'd you recognize us?" I asked in jest.

"Number one, you're tall. Number two, your hair's long on top and short in back, the opposite of mine," he laughed. He was wearing tight jeans and ankle-high boots. To me he was the perfect urban hipster. His dark eyes twinkled. His mouth couldn't decide whether to turn down or up. I could feel his energy. I liked him the minute I saw him.

Allan introduced us to his wife, Linda, a dazzling beauty with big blue eyes and long blond hair curling around her neck and over one shoulder. She was wearing a loose-knit dress. Then he introduced a guy named Alexi and his girlfriend, Nina. From Nina's accent, I knew she was American; and when Alexi called for a waiter, I heard he was fluent in Greek. Allan explained to them how I'd just come from the U.S. with the Air Force. Alexi poured me a bit of something in a small glass, laughing at the face I made with my first sip.

"Never had absinthe?" Alexi asked. I shook my head. "You know the Greek word it comes from? *Apsinthion*. It means undrinkable." Everybody laughed as I made a face and spit it back into the glass.

"Here," he said, "some white wine to wash it down. And there's water if you want."

"Alexi's from here," said Allan. "His father works at Athens College with me."

I introduced Barker as a deejay at the base radio station. Alexi said he relied on that station for good music and clinked glasses with Barker. Alexi was broad-shouldered and handsome, with thick brown wavy hair. His pinstriped shirt and sleeveless sweater said educated upper class. Nina was tall and thin with her long hair pulled back. Her serious eyes focused on each of us as we spoke, taking everything in.

The six of us were crowded around two little round tables pulled together in a figure eight. Linda was the one who lit up the group, her blue eyes framed with long lashes and perfect eyebrows, her full lips forming staccato bursts of words and smiles around lovely teeth. I had met few such charismatic, gorgeous charmers. Her conversation tumbled out at a blue-streak New York pace, perfectly formed and funny.

"Welcome to Athens, Steve," she said and clinked her glass with mine. "You are not the average military guy I expected, is he, Allan? No, not at all, no kidding, you're softer and shyer. When Allan said you were an officer, I pictured ramrod straight, chin you could thresh wheat on, eyes, you know, like a raptor, but you look like an artist or something. Are you?"

I paused. "Well, I was in graduate school in literature when they drafted me. I've always liked writing. And I discovered a terrific artist on the Mississippi coast at my last posting."

"Drafted you?" asked Allan. "I didn't think you could get drafted into the Air Force."

I gave them a brief version of my odyssey so far — being picked up hitchhiking and switching from the Army, the year in Biloxi with civil rights workers and military resisters, the letters from Deborah on Crete, and my conning of the assignment process to come here.

"Well, Allan, you picked the right guy to help you dub that film," said Linda, "that just sounded like a movie in the making, didn't it, already cast, the star right here, I can't wait to see it!" The group laughed.

Alexi said, "Let's hope the rest of your time in Athens is as interesting as that. Maybe you can stay on when you get discharged; Allan can hook you up with a production crew and you can star in your own film."

"I'm just glad there's room in the service for people like you and your friends who can resist the military," Linda said. "Thanks to the Air Force, you're here with us now. A toast: to Steve!"

*What a group*, I thought. *I'm so lucky.*


Allan outlined for me what dubbing a film entailed. It sounded pretty easy. He gave me a little map and an address where I should meet him that Saturday. I liked his gravelly voice and the way a blazing grin could transform his features as if turned on by a switch. We'd arrived at about half past ten, and there were now many empty bottles and glasses on our table. My watch said ten till two.

We got up to leave, and I looked up to see Nina staring at me. Falling into step with me, she took my arm and said softly, "You're sad, aren't you?" I felt naked and accused. No one had ever been that direct with me, especially a stranger. I was borderline drunk, but she seemed sharp and smooth. "What are you sad about?" she asked when I didn't answer, as we walked behind everybody else toward an intersection.

"I don't know," I said. I didn't want to concede that I was a sad guy, but I knew I wasn't as comfortable and happy as most of our group seemed, except for Nina. "My girlfriend isn't here" was the first thing that popped into my mind. "She got a scholarship to the American University in Paris just as I arrived from the States."

"Bet it's more than just your girlfriend," she said. "It's not a happy place right now, Greece." I felt Nina had X-rayed me. I turned it over in my mind. Was I sad? I was trying to straddle two worlds, being the new officer on the base and a new citizen of downtown Athens and its expatriates who had no one to answer to. Straddling two worlds made me feel like less than a full member of either, which was what I'd been doing in Austin and Biloxi for the last eighteen months. I didn't like feeling like a visitor, or an actor in two divergent plays. I wanted so much to be in the thick of a committed and meaningful life, bringing to the table all that I had and was, with deep friendships and comrades working for something wonderful. The U.S. and the world were burning with violence. I wanted to help put out the flames.

Barker and I bade the group good-night and sank into the VW for the trip back to the base. "That's great about the film with Allan," he said. "Keep that connection going. He's a cool guy."

The next day, at the radio station, I heard the Rolling Stones' anthems about revolution and chaos back in the world, "Street Fighting Man" and "Sympathy for the Devil."

"Can't play those babies on the air," Barker said. "Way too hot."

I went off-base for lunch to a fish-and-chips place. I wanted to sit alone and take stock of my new acquaintances and opportunities. Great new friends, even if Barker's hipster hype got on my nerves. Through him, I had met Allan and Linda. I visited the Gobbler from time to time. I learned her name was Solange.

\* \* \*

Al Citron called me over one day when we were the only ones in the office. "You know, Colonel Fisher warns everybody to stay away from certain people on the streets." He glanced into my eyes, kind but serious. "He does that not because guys might catch something. It's because they don't have any idea who she is. And guys can get in over their heads."

I nodded. "Thanks, Al. I appreciate that."

"You know, my landlord has a daughter. I told him about you, and he said she'd like to go out with an American." He put his business card on my desk, with his landlord's name and number on it. I took it but thought, *Just what I need, a date with Al's landlord's daughter.* I tossed the card away.

\* \* \*

Buzzing farther and faster around the streets and boulevards of Athens a couple of days later, my mind humming with thoughts about Greece and my eyes on the dial of the car radio trying to tune in "Everyday People," another Sly Stone hit, I turned left across the busiest street near the base. I had time only to slam on the brakes and wham! A guy coming the other way smashed into my right front fender. My elbows hit the steering wheel and my face hit my knuckles in a burst of pain. My glasses snapped in two. It took a minute to get my breath. I barely heard the other driver yelling at me in Greek and a cop asking for my license. I was swallowing blood from a cut inside my mouth. The

Greek guy got belligerent, waving his arms, and the cop pushed him away from me. My elbows were aching and swelling up. All I could think was *Man, what a fuckup. I lost my concentration. Now I'm going to lose my mobility.*

That week, Colonel Bert gave me the Eight-Ball Award for having an accident. It became a popular story. Somebody from the base newspaper had been tipped off and took a picture of the commander handing me a 16-pound "left-handed bowling ball" with a white eight painted on it. "Left-handed" emphasized the insult, I guess. The *Stars and Stripes* military newspaper picked up the picture and ran it all over Europe.

SPARE THE THOUGHT—Lt. Col. Bert Fisher, CO of the 2140th Communications Sq, Athens, Greece, presents 2nd Lt. Stephen Larner, vehicle control officer, with the "8-Ball" award which he earned with his POV accident. The award, a left-handed, five-fingered 16-pound bowling ball is given to anyone who has a reportable accident and stays with the violator until someone else has an accident. —Air Force Photo

"Sorry, Steve, but we have to take your license while we work it out with the police. You're gonna have to take a safety course, too," Captain Al said. "Is everything OK, guy? You seem a little preoccupied lately."

Oh yeah, I was preoccupied. Everything I wanted to do lay outside the base. Nothing I wanted to do lay inside the base, except work in the radio station, which was not in my job description or pay grade. I would have gladly taken a pay cut if they'd let me trade straight-up with Barker: I'll play the records and give the news and you can report to the colonel about the broadband channels.

When I was at the station the next time, Barker comforted me about the car accident. "Everybody's had one," he said. "The streets are crazy. I had mine. Just move on, Steve."

"What happened to you?"

"One night about dusk I hit an old man jaywalking across the street. You know, wearing all black, no streetlights, like these idiots do," he said as he cued up a record. "Just a minute." He shifted his voice lower and did a station break.

"What happened to the old man?"

"Killed him."

"What?! So what did his family do? What came of it?"

"No idea. I didn't even get a ticket. Hold on, let me give the time here." He announced the time and closed the switch to the mike and pushed it away, leaning back in his squeaky captain's chair. "If it's dark and you're wearing black, you're asking for it. Specially if you can't walk good. Wasn't my fault. I just needed to keep it off my record."

"So did you pay anything to his family, or…"

"Nah. The base police fixed it for me. It never happened."

I had no comment to that. I left the studio and went home. I sat on the porch in the dark and wondered how I'd handle it if someone like Barker killed my old friend, my elderly landlord, Mr. Petros. I hated the fact that Barker was one of the only two friends I had on the base. But I didn't want to lose him. Radio and the music pouring out of the U.S. were in my blood.

* * *

The next weekend I auditioned for the dubbing job, reading some hokey dialogue right out of "Gunsmoke." In ten minutes, they said I had the part; they were behind schedule and wanted to start the dubbing right away. The directors were two large and pudgy guys in turtleneck cashmere sweaters, named Max Roman and James Paris.

It was a small operation, loops of film hanging on the wall like fan belts at a mechanic's shop, two expensive Nagra reel-to-reel tape recorders, microphones set up with foam baffles on them, egg cartons lining the walls and ceiling to deaden the sound. The film was a sort of "Wagon Train" western called *Seven Guns for El Gringo* in this English version we were creating. It was shot with a European cast chosen for their faces and speaking whatever language they wanted to in the filming; dubbers shaped it into French, Italian, Spanish and English versions. A Spanish version called *Siete Muertos Para El Tejano* toured the U.S. Southwest.

I voiced the lines for El Gringo. After the first few lines of rehearsal, with Allan playing an older, crustier posse member who advised the "Young Elvis"–looking El Gringo, Max Roman gently held my shoulder and said, "You have a leetle Texas accent? Allan says you can make eet even more Texas, okay?"

Over the next week Allan and I stood side by side at the microphones, inventing and modifying American speech to fit the characters' mouth movements as each silent clip rolled on a screen in front of us. Max and James gave us a generic English translation, typed on index cards, of what the characters were supposed to be saying, but it never matched the mouth movements and gestures, which is why it took fifteen minutes or so to dub one short line of dialogue. First, we'd see their silent mouth rhythms. It was hard to keep my memory from supplying TV commercial jingles that fit the singing scenes. Allan cracked up.

"No, don't start," he said close to my ear. "These guys are on a tight budget and tight schedule. Please don't make me laugh. We'll never get out of here!"

Over two weeks of dubbing, three or four hours a day, the film cowboys Brooklyn Allan and Texas Steve became living versions of the older/younger characters we were playing. We'd both grown up with our TV evenings full of shoot-'em-up allegories like "Have Gun, Will Travel," "The Rifleman," and "Gunsmoke." There was a rousing, rugged song to fill a long scene as the posse rode into a canyon. Max and James were worried about it. Allan named it "Wait for the Wagon," and smoothly improvised various lines to fit, telling me about his folk-singing experience in Greenwich Village during breaks.

We wound up singing "Wait for the Wagon" later that night at a bar near the studio. Allan told a couple of Greek guys getting loaded at the bar, "We're folksingers from America. We just put that song out in the U.S. as a record." They bought us a round of retsina, put arms around our shoulders, and sang "Waaay Foda Wayonn" with us about five times.

In our last dubbing session, we worked over and over on a difficult scene that apparently touched a nerve with James and Max. Despite being the new guy without any experience, I suddenly figured the dialogue out after about twenty failed takes. I made up: "You know the law is always crooked." They didn't like it. I suggested the Dylan line that came to me first, "To live outside the law you must be honest." They both fit, but no, no. Allan came to my defense and it got uncomfortable.

James wound up yelling that the line was bad. "No politics, I told you Allan," he said. Allan yelled back.

Max took Allan and me by the shoulders and marched us toward the door. "We cannot risk thees on the tape," he whispered to us. "Please understand and now go take a break. I talk to James."

"OK," Allan said.

"What was that about?" I said when we were out on the sidewalk.

"Ahh, don't worry about it. They're just temperamental artists. Hey, here's a flyer about a play I'm doing at the school, *Zoo Story*. Come and read for it. I've got you penciled in to do one of the roles, it's a two-man play. Look, I gotta run, Linda's waiting dinner. Call me if you want to talk it over. Tell Max we're done for the day."

My car was still being repaired and I was still on driving probation for my accident. I caught a cab home and wandered in a daze through the forest of rosebushes and orange trees in my yard. Wow, I thought, I just dubbed a movie, and I really like Allan. Lying in the grass with my head against the citron tree, looking up at the sky full of stars, I dropped off to sleep right there. I had a really sweet dream in which everyone I met wanted to show me a new part of Paris, which they called "Nuevo Parees." Deborah slipped out of sight around every corner I came to. James Paris kept coming into the scene saying "No politics!"

# ELEVEN

In my mail slot at the squadron mail room, I found what I had been waiting months for: a thin blue airmail envelope with oval-shaped lettering! I ripped it open. Finally, a letter from Deborah in Paris!

"Dear Stephanos," it started. "November in Paris is cold and wet. I have a room on the fifth floor of a house built in the 1840s in St. Germain. It's a garret room about 3 by 5 meters. Just my size, eh? Toilet is down a floor. If you really have to go bad you use a pot with a lid from the flea market and empty it when you can get into the real 'bathroom,' which is a toilet and sink. Luckily I have three friends who say I can shower at their places. One is Philippe, but his place is too far from the American University. The other two are girls from the U. who are only three or four blocks away.

"I spend most of my time outside of classes at this coffee place at the edge of the Latin Quarter, east of St. Germain. I got run over when the cops herded people into an alleyway during the riots, so I'm not climbing stairs unless I have to."

She went on about the piles of reading she was having to do in a full load of English and American Lit classes and how old-school the profs were, except that one had taken a shine to her writing and recommended her to another professor. Then came the bad news: "I'm having to join the family in Rome for Christmas. Dom is insisting on it as it may be the last family vacation together. So I won't see you unless you can come to Rome, and then it won't be just us but *la familia Italiana militaria*, the full catastrophe."

*Well, fuck. So near, so far.* I folded the letter, put it in my pocket and checked out for lunch. This bohemian fling I'd been expecting to have with Deb had just receded farther into the future. Made me wonder when we'd get time to hang out together without the octopus of the family and my job as communications officer.

November was getting chilly and damp in Athens, too, and when Allan and Linda invited me for Thanksgiving dinner, it was cold enough that I could see my breath as I hiked up the steep part of Dafnomili Street to their apartment. Hanging up my lightweight Air Force jacket, I admired Allan's Navy pea coat.

"Hey, I'll get you one if you want. There are these stalls down in Piraeus by the port. They've got tons of Navy surplus stuff. We can go tomorrow if you want."

I was all for it. I was also all for the traditional American Thanksgiving dinner Linda prepared. Alexi and Nina were there, from our first meeting in Kolonaki in August, and a Greek couple named Yannis and Dora. Everybody was in fine spirits, taking turns telling stories of recent adventures. We had glass after glass of retsina and Mateus rosé wine and made repeated toasts. Allan told them about our film-dubbing job and we sang "Wait for the Wagon" for them. Linda was radiant. It was hard for me to keep my eyes off her gorgeous, mobile face. The biggest toast came when she announced she was pregnant, and of course she, Nina and Dora began talking excitedly as we poured more wine and toasted the new parents-to-be. I was thrilled for them. They were the first close friends I'd ever had who expected a baby.

Alexi switched smoothly from English to Greek, translating for me and Nina when the conversation with Dora and Yannis got animated. Yannis was some kind of a writer and Dora was a clothing designer, that much I got; but when he and Alexi engaged in dialogues, I got the feeling that Alexi didn't put it all into English. I wondered what their pauses meant — with a raised eyebrow and poker-face monosyllables standing out a bit in the general gaiety.

The next day I met Allan at Constitution Square, and we took a taxi down to Piraeus, a funky extension of Athens, with stevedores and sailors and cheap cafés to fuel them up. We walked through the sidewalks, jammed with kiosks selling magazines and newspapers, hundreds of varieties of gum, key chains, worry beads and crosses. Stuff lined the walls of kiosks that were not much bigger than phone booths, the proprietor reaching out through a tiny window, like a bird in a cage, to take money and make change. The cuisine climbed the economic scale from stalls with lamb skewers and fried potatoes made on a single burner to places big enough for two adults and two kids to work elbow to elbow serving paper plates of chopped octopus with thyme and basil sticking to chunks of feta cheese, as well as selling huge jars of olive oil, pyramids of retsina bottles, and votive candles. There were stalls with tools, with clothes, with antique clocks and watches and toys, pots and pans and china and glass figurines.

"Don't you just love it?" said Allan, his face aglow. "And there's a market near the Acropolis, at Monastiraki, with even more stuff than this — real antiques and art. We'll go there soon. So what do you hear from Deb?" Allan asked.

"She says she's not coming to Athens for Christmas after all,"
I said. "Her parents are going to Rome, and she'll meet them there,
then try to come here. But probably not."

"Oh, no! That's a drag," Allan said. "Are you okay about that?"

"No. It is a drag. I was sure hoping to see her," I said. "I was
hoping she could enjoy a night with your friends, like that super
Thanksgiving dinner at your place."

We turned into an aisle of stalls specializing in military surplus
clothes: racks and mounds of pea coats, wool uniforms, hats and
slickers from the Greek Navy and the American Navy. I got a pea coat
from Nikolás, the guy who sold Allan his. Those double-breasted,
quarter-inch-thick wool coats were sharper than anything we had in
the Air Force. I could turn the four-inch-wide collar up and feel like I
was in a World War II movie with Allan, Richard Widmark and
Humphrey Bogart. I loved that you could take on new looks here.
El Gringo joins the Navy.

We wandered back toward the taxi stands. "It's been a wild year
in Paris," Allan said. "Deborah must have seen the French doing
revolution again. They're great at it! You know what," he said, "there's
a party you should come to. The Christmas party at the embassy.
Are you guys from the base invited?"

I said I had heard about it, but I'd been spending almost no time
around the base after working hours, so I hadn't heard any details.

"Look, I'm going," said Allan, "and I know the USIS people
there, so I'll call and make sure you're on the guest list. Sure, that's
perfect, I don't know why I hadn't thought about it. Barker will be
there. He's the DJ for those occasions. Didn't he tell you about it?"

"You know, I haven't seen him much since he told me that story
about killing that pedestrian."

"Oh. Yeah, that was cold. But you've gotta come, Steve. You need a party if Deborah's not gonna be here." We stopped at a stall with the fragrance of freshly roasting chicken pouring out of it.

"Amerìci?" The vendor asked.

"Ne, ne," Allan said, "We're Ammies." The guy pointed to a *Time* magazine cover of Elvis in his Army uniform serving in Germany that he had taped to his wall.

"Jail House Rocking!" the man grinned. "Blue Suede Shoes, no?" He leaned back and rotated his pelvis, laughing.

We gave him a thumb's up and walked on. "So who goes to embassy parties here?" I asked Allan.

"Everybody in the American military scene, and lots of their Greek friends. It's the whole diplomatic crowd from all over Athens. The whole eastern Mediterranean, actually. People like to visit Athens from Italy, Turkey. You've got to come, OK?"

A couple of days before Christmas, I was ready for a party. The officers had invited me to various Christmas Eve or Christmas-day gatherings at their houses, but the embassy party with Allan was the one I wanted to see most.

I wore my dress-blue uniform, fitted tighter at the waist than a standard suit, with five silver buttons and square shoulders with epaulets, where you attached your silver or gold officer insignia. I had just been given the automatic promotion to first lieutenant from second, and I was proud that the new silver bar on each shoulder signified that I was not a complete newbie. The uniform effect was powerful. Even when I thought about how much I distrusted the military and how many civilians would ridicule the military symbolism, I found that wearing this full-dress outfit felt good. The tan short-sleeve uniform we wore daily on the base made me look skinnier. It had no style points. Silver buttons on a fitted jacket, though, with a well-tied

Windsor knot in the dark blue tie, was cool for me. At this point I still appreciated the status conferred by the officer-and-a-gentleman look.

I had my car back and was cleared to drive for good behavior. I parked a couple of blocks away and walked up to the four-story stone embassy building in the Psychico district north of downtown. The guards held me up at the front door because they couldn't find me on the guest list, but Allan came down and told them I was his guest.

The party was in the second-floor ballroom, and there was Barker serving as deejay. About equal numbers of people were dressed in uniform and in civilian clothes. There were the dark-green dress suits of Army officers, the double-breasted dark blue of the Navy, with gold stripes on the sleeve down by the wrist, and epaulets on the captains. A Navy captain was equivalent to an Air Force colonel, and there were several of them there, being fawned over by lesser ranks. Two or three other Air Force guys were dressed like I was, but I only knew them in passing. Barker had his jazz-show records there, mostly Sinatra, Ella, Bobby Darin's big-band tunes, Bill Evans' piano music. Greek waiters in short white captain's table jackets circulated with trays of hors d'oeuvres and wine glasses, taking orders for cocktails. Long tables at both ends of the room were piled with Greek food, roast beef, and carved turkeys with trimmings. Allan had on a sport coat with an ascot in his open collar, hair slicked back and mustache trimmed. I asked if Linda was there.

"No, she's getting that nausea pregnancy brings, and besides, she's been to all these bashes since we've been here."

He introduced me to several people in the diplomatic corps, whose names and faces didn't stick with me until I met one guy, named Bob Wozniak, who was especially warm with Allan.

"Steve here's new to the base. We've already dubbed a movie, and he's going to be in a play with me," Allan said.

"Well, you couldn't have picked a better guy to show you around," Wozniak said to me. In that wine-induced glow of loud-talking pleasantries, I wondered who Wozniak was. He was balding, had a neat pencil mustache, smelled of after-shave, and looked like a professor in his blue button-down shirt, striped tie and tweedy sports jacket.

"What do you do here, Bob?" I asked.

"I'm just a USIS staffer," he said.

"So what do they have you doing?"

"Matter of fact," he said, "I've just set up a tour for Allan to play his folk music at USIS libraries and U.S. installations. He'll be going to Rome, Brindisi, Thessaloniki, let's see, to a couple of the islands, then finish at Crete."

"No kidding, at Crete?" I asked Allan.

"Yes, I'm going to Iraklion Base on New Year's Eve. Maybe I'll meet Deborah's folks."

A guy who seemed to know Wozniak well came up, shook his hand, nodded at Allan and me, and said he was going to ask Barker to play a request. He held a record album under his arm. His face was flushed and sweating. Too much ouzo punch, or maybe the shots of Chivas Regal and Johnny Walker Red available free at the executive bar.

Wozniak tilted his head to see the album, asking what it was. The guy showed it to us — the soundtrack from *Phaedra*, the film with Anthony Perkins and Melina Mercouri. A hit in 1962, it was a modern adaptation of the Euripides story about Phaedra, who seduces her own stepson, Alexis. In the modern version, Alexis is Tony Perkins and his father is an extremely wealthy shipping tycoon whose second wife is the young, fiery Phaedra, played by Melina Mercouri. Alexis and Phaedra have an affair. I had seen it and liked it. I started saying how much I liked the music when Wozniak cut in:

"Not a good idea, Frank. Don't." But Frank was plowing through the crowd toward Barker, who cheerfully reached for the album to put it on when Wozniak caught up to them.

"What's the deal?" I asked Allan, as we followed Wozniak up to Barker. Wozniak was saying something into Barker's ear as the pounding minor chords of the film music started playing, the last three notes of each measure going down the scale like trouble brewing. I liked it — it sounded tragically Middle Eastern, romantic and doomed. There was a popping sound as Barker lifted the needle from the record, put it aside, and slipped a Tony Bennett record in its place. Frank started loudly complaining to Barker, but Wozniak took him by the arm and steered him off to the side, where the argument continued for a minute until Wozniak opened a door, hauled the guy inside an office, and shut the door. A few people turned to follow that exit with their eyes, but nobody paid any more attention to it.

"What was that about?" I asked Allan. He took me by the elbow and we walked back along the edge of the festivities toward one of the food tables.

"Well, Steve-o," he said quietly, smiling at people we passed, "that film score was written by Mikis Theodorakis. Not only written, but played and conducted by Mikis, who has been declared an enemy of the state by the Colonels. It's against the law to play his music in Greece, even in your own home. He's the most famous composer in Greece. He even directs the Athens Little Symphony. He's sort of their Leonard Bernstein. And, to double the trouble, Melina Mercouri is Theodorakis's close friend and collaborator. She's on the poster for the movie back in the States, but it won't play here. The Colonels will see to that. She's a well-known leftist, like Mikis. Bob had to stop the album because it would have been a major diplomatic faux pas. There are bound to be informers for the Colonels in this ballroom."

At the buffet, we piled up roast beef and pasta salad on our plates. We found a sofa and sat down. A waiter brought us glasses of white wine. We ate and sipped, as Allan scanned the room.

"Well, it's just the political reality here," Allan said, keeping a smile on his face as he scanned the room. "Somebody at the front door should have noticed that record and confiscated it."

"Isn't an embassy like a piece of U.S. soil?"

"Yup. It is. But you don't wave red flags at bulls." We went and got chocolate cake and coffee for dessert and sat down again.

"Think we'll see Wozniak again tonight?" I asked Allan.

"Maybe. He should be around."

"What did you say he did here?"

"Technically, he's cultural affairs staffer for the USIS. But everybody knows he's CIA," said Allan in a low voice.

"CIA? And he set up your tour?"

"Yup. He likes me and my music."

"What do you sing?"

"Dylan. Leonard Cohen. Woody Guthrie. Pete Seeger."

"But…they're all political. Why can you sing Dylan or Pete Seeger on Crete?"

"Bob's heard my whole show. He's never told me what to sing or what not to sing," Allan said with satisfaction.

"What does the CIA get out of helping you sing left-wing folk songs?"

"Compare me to the Colonels. Or to Islamic regimes. Folk music makes the U.S. look like the champion of freedom, while it also sticks the knife into some of our hypocrisies. Maybe not everybody gets all the English, but it's a win-win for Uncle Sam."

"So you're — you're a Trojan horse!"

"Yes!" Allan said, and dissolved in a big guffaw. "I never thought of it in that image before. Wow! The subversive little ideas climbing out of my guitar, infecting minds! That's great, Steve-o. Thank you."

I had worried that my first Christmas away from home might be hard to handle. Christmases had been forced and grim since my parents divorced five years earlier, and fragments of the family had to get together at various times or various days during the season to keep the peace. But I felt comfortable here at the U.S. Embassy in the police state of Greece, with Barker playing jazz and a few Christmas tunes in jazzy versions. I wanted to know more about this cultural chess game.

"Tell me some more about the Colonels," I asked Allan.

"Not here," he said. "Where's your car?"

"Two blocks down, toward town."

"OK," said Allan. "You go there. Then ten minutes later, I'll go. See you at your car in ten minutes."

Sitting in my VW, Allan said, "If anybody comes up to us say we're waiting for our wives from the embassy. If they don't understand English let me handle them."

He told me that Linda and he had come to Greece in 1963 and the Colonels staged their coup in 1967, at three in the morning. They sent out squads with lists and arrested 10,000 people by morning. There had been a lot of push-pull between the right wing and the various left-wing parties. The king, the son of the old king, was new, and all he knew was to kowtow to the right wing and the military. Most people woke up that morning and said, "Well, let's give 'em a go and see if they can keep order."

"Didn't anybody resist?"

"Some did, and wound up in island jails. One guy got shot, ironically a black American who didn't stop when they said to. But the secret police had been so active here, going all the way back to the thirties. They'd infiltrated and beat down all the organized resistance.

The Colonels were from the security forces, and they'd been in power just over a year before you came in August. They've banned everything western: rock music, American movies, miniskirts, most modern writers. Lots of people in the arts and literary communities have left. Most go to Paris."

"So that's what was bothering James Paris at the film dub job? And that's not his real name?"

"Who knows his real name! But yeah, you can't mention 'the law' in anything. I just got caught up in the dubbing and forgot the politics there."

When cars came by with their lights shining in on us, we pretended to be tourists, holding up an unfolded city map in front of our faces. I asked Allan if the U.S. had a role in the coup.

"Oh, I don't think it could have happened without the CIA's approval."

"What about the rest of Europe? My commander told me we're the southeastern flank of NATO."

"The Colonels used a NATO counterinsurgency plan to do it! The plan was named — get this — Prometheus." We shook our heads at the sad irony. I realized my position here as a U.S. officer could be dangerous.

Allan said that everything here is framed as Christians versus Communists, even though the most the communist parties ever got was fifteen percent of the vote. Then headlights approached us and stopped in front of my car. Allan looked out the passenger side window and waved, saying "Yassou" and something else in Greek.

"Here they come," he said. "Be cool." There were two thin, young cops wearing light-blue uniforms with epaulets and high-peaked police hats. One came to Allan's side and the other to mine, each shining flashlights in on us. Allan shifted into charming, smiling Greek. *Thank*

*God he's an actor,* I thought. He jerked his thumb my way and I caught the words "militár" and "embassy." Then he was holding up the city map and pointing to it, asking for their guidance, gesturing with his hands with each word, his brows pinched together, worrying, mentioning souvlaki, oktopodaki. *Ah, he's asking about restaurants.* The guy on Allan's side leaned in and circled a couple of places on the map, and they babbled about food and drink for a while. The two cops looked about 25. They flicked off their flashlights, touched their swooped-up caps, and said a polite "kali niktasas," good night, gentlemen.

"Just local traffic cops," Allan said. "I told them we were stumped about where to take our wives to get good Greek food for dinner, and they were eager to help. The security cops, now, are older and trickier. Let's drive back toward the embassy — less chance of them harassing us there. Then you should go home on that other main street to the west. Enough intrigue for one night!"

At the embassy corner, Allan got out, shut the door and leaned in the window. "It's been great tonight, Steve. I'm glad I thought of asking you. Hope you didn't miss Deb too much."

"I didn't. It was interesting as hell, Allan. Good night."

"I think you ought to use taxis when you come to town, whenever you can. Less conspicuous that way. Get some body shop to take those flower decals off. OK, buddy, I'll call you in early January and we'll set up rehearsals for *Zoo Story,* OK?"

I drove home thinking, *Best damn Christmas I've had in years.*

# TWELVE

Allan and I sit facing each other in folding chairs on a raised pro-
scenium stage. It's four in the afternoon, early in February, 1969. The
auditorium is dark and empty in the Hellenic-American Union in
downtown Athens. The stage is lit by one bank of lights. We are doing
our first read-through of Edward Albee's *Zoo Story*.

The first words in the play are Allan's. He plays a tragic loner
named Jerry.

Jerry: "I've been to the zoo. I said, I've been to the zoo. *MISTER,
I'VE BEEN TO THE ZOO!*"

My character, Peter, is sitting on a park bench and hoping this
guy isn't talking to him. I look up:

"Hm?...What?...I'm sorry, were you talking to me?"

Jerry: "I went to the zoo, and then I walked until I came here.
Have I been walking north?"

A weirdo has accosted a mild-mannered office worker. A few
lines later, Jerry makes the conflict clear.

Jerry: "Do you mind if we talk?"

Peter: [obviously minding] "Why…no, no."

Jerry: "Yes you do; you do."

Peter: [puts his book down, his pipe out and away, smiling] "No, really; I don't mind."

Jerry: "Yes, you do."

Allan, a veteran of many plays, is projecting an aggressive edge from the first lines. The play is all dialogue between Allan's angry, desperate, manipulative loner and my naïve and meek guy. This was no film dubbing, where Allan's old codger and my El Gringo were on equal terms. Allan had performed El Gallo in *The Fantasticks,* directed *Billy Liar* and *Look Back in Anger,* and I'd only had bit parts in light stuff and musicals like *Threepenny Opera, A Christmas Carol, Trial by Jury, Once Upon a Mattress.* It was exhilarating, and scary, sitting across from Allan, hearing his vocal skills embody Jerry's street persona. My character, Peter, seems passive but shares control of the pace, making Jerry try every wheedling trick he has to keep Peter interested.

"Where did you learn all these verbal riffs?" I asked Allan when we took a break.

"I guess in the subways, the streets," he said. "In Greenwich Village I had to hustle my way onto the stages when some pretty powerful guys auditioned every night in every hole-in-the-wall club. My friend Lenny and I played gigs at The Commons with Dave Van Ronk and Tom Paxton. We called ourselves the Serendipity Singers." He chuckled at the name. "Then we were The Highwaymen. We shared a stage once with Ramblin' Jack Elliott and Bob Dylan. My girlfriend at the time was black and it was cool, mostly, but we had to talk our way past some nasty guys at times, both black and white."

But as suddenly as they had found an audience doing a regular Friday-night gig at The Bitter End, Allan and Lenny lost it when the owner told them, "Sorry, guys, but next Friday I gotta make room for

Noel and Friends." Noel was Noel Stookey, who started going by his
middle name, Paul, to harmonize with his friends, Peter and Mary.

"They were a supergroup formed by Dylan's manager, Albert
Grossman, who rehearsed them for six weeks. So there went our
Greenwich Village career," Allan said. "That's when Linda and I
decided to come to Athens. We saw a little ad in the paper: 'Interviews for Athens College.' I got hired on the spot and we started
packing for Europe."

Every afternoon after work at the base, I went downtown to the
Hellenic American Union. We rehearsed alone in the empty auditorium for eight weeks. As Jerry forces himself into Peter's space,
our voices rose and echoed in the hall. Jerry's anger and desperation
became more intense, a mental boxing match. It was exhausting to
keep my eyes and ears on the domineering Jerry, staying vulnerable
while keeping my guard up. I watched for an opening, but Peter never
got to land a punch at all. I had to wait, and wait, as the rising adren-

alin of a fight wound both of us tighter and tighter. Allan told me, "Jerry really assaults Peter, verbally and then literally, at the end. You might not want to go as far as this script goes, Steve. I hope you do, but anytime you want out, say so."

Jerry is single and lives on the fourth floor of a rooming house in half a room, separated from the other half by panel board. He lives his bleak life as if it's in Dante's Inferno, each floor of the building inhabited by somebody caught in a different kind of suffering: a woman Jerry has never seen who cries all the time, a black queen who plucks his eyebrows "with Buddhist concentration" and hogs the bathroom, a disgusting landlady. Allan's face grew taut and red and his eyes flared as he spat out Albee's description of the landlady: "a fat, ugly, mean, stupid, unwashed, misanthropic, cheap, drunken *bag of garbage!*"

Allan stopped to correct my reactions: "Don't sympathize with this guy! He's a scheming manipulator, Steve, he's a mess. Peter is appalled by this guy."

"It's hard," I said, "being as passive as Peter is."

"I know. But you've got to be Peter the way he's written, or it won't work. Jerry's trying to make Peter understand loneliness and suffering with his stories about the pain of the people in his building, the zoo animals isolated in their cages, and the people on the streets that you, Peter, are more comfortable *not* having to think about."

Jerry accuses Peter of being a powerless wimp living in a female-dominated household, where taking care of parakeets and cats is as bold as he ever gets. I feel Peter's physical fear. My shoulders go up defensively. My armpits stink after each rehearsal.

In the final sequence, Jerry tries one last way to get through to Peter. He starts by tickling him, then punches him on the arm and pushes him to the ground. He seizes the moment and challenges Peter to "fight for your bench" and pulls out a switchblade that he throws on the ground between them. Jerry grabs Peter and slaps him each time he snarls the word "fight:" "You fight, you miserable bastard; *fight* for that bench; *fight* for your parakeets; *fight* for your cats, *fight* for your two daughters; *fight* for your life; fight for your *manhood,* you pathetic little vegetable!"

Allan's hair flies in strands off his high, wet forehead, saliva hitting me in the face. Finally Peter accepts Jerry's absurd framing of their encounter and mobilizes his strength to fight back, though he doesn't know how. I grab the open switchblade and hold it awkwardly in front of me at arm's length, shaking all over. Jerry says quietly, "All right, so be it," and runs onto the blade.

Even though our stage knife had a retractable blade, it was a searing moment for us both. The stage in those days, and movies also, hadn't yet been filled with violence and blood as they are today. The ending was shocking: Peter, frozen in disgust, with Jerry draped over his outstretched arm, the knife buried in Jerry's stomach, Allan's wet hair against my arms and chest. Jerry collapses and says up to me, gently, "Thank you, Peter... I was afraid I'd drive you away. I came unto you, and you have comforted me. Dear Peter."

This is a spine-tingling climax, but there is another shocker: we only get to do the dress rehearsal, in front of the technical crew and about twenty of Allan's colleagues, after two months of rehearsals. It is now early April. The dress rehearsal has gone great, without a hitch. The last line is mine, and I deliver it in a howl after running off into the wings: "*Oh my GOD!*" Allan and I are surprised when the little audience gives us a whistling, standing ovation. We take bows with our arms around each other. But the next night — opening night — with people standing outside the box office waiting to buy tickets an hour before curtain, Allan comes rushing backstage, his eyes darting back and forth, his brow furrowed.

He says he's caught between two moral dilemmas and needs to know what I want to do. "The first one is, the publisher of the play called and is withholding permission to perform it here. Albee and Arthur Miller have signed an open letter in *The New York Times* forbidding their work to be produced in Greece because of the Colonels. Dilemma number two is that, if we cancel it, I'm betraying all of your work with me. You've taken eight weeks of Jerry's abuse, and I love you like a brother. If I obey Albee's letter, I take away your performance from you. Christ! What to do!" He turned in a circle, running both hands through his hair, leaving them on the back on his head, his elbows splayed out. *"What do we do, Steve?"*

I didn't hesitate. "We don't do it," I say. "We don't do it. Look, I'm more sorry for you than for me. You produced and directed it. It was gonna be your students and faculty buddies in the audience. No; we just can't do it." It hurts to say that. But insulting Albee by going ahead? No.

Allan grabs me in a hug. "Oh, man, that's what I want to do, too. Steve, I'm so proud of both of us right now! Thank you. Thank you for everything!"

We stood there, adrenaline racing but not sure what we should do next. Allan switched into a Bogart imitation, adapting the famous line from *Casablanca:* "I guess we'll always have the dress rehearsal!"

Then, the dilemma of what to do for the audiences that had already bought tickets, several hundred of them. We put up a sign saying that tonight's opening performance was postponed until Sunday. We went to the Hilton's coffee shop that night — Allan, Linda, me, and Jack, a writer friend of Allan's visiting from Berkeley. In those days, the Hilton Hotel was an island of Americana that appealed to the whole European expatriate scene as a progressive place to see and be seen. The Athens Hilton hosted concerts and talks by scholars. There was no access in Athens to American pop culture besides Armed

Forces Radio and the Hilton. You went to the Hilton for hamburgers and chocolate cake, drip coffee and bacon-and-egg breakfasts, as well as late-night liaisons, as I had done earlier with Jean.

So the *Zoo Story* team got coffee and shots of cognac and brainstormed how to replace the play. We decided to put on a poetry reading about U.S. democratic traditions. We threw it together in the next two days. I called Deborah's father on Crete and told him what had happened and that I really wanted to get hold of Deb. He gave me a phone number that he said was not in her room but somewhere in her building.

"We've never called her there," he said. "She called and said we could call that number if there was an emergency."

I called the number, leaving a message with the person who answered that the play was off and we were improvising a poetry reading. "Tell her to come to Athens," I told the guy.

The next night, she called back. "Stéfanos! Poetry and ouzo tonight!"

"Deborah!" I yelled. "Where are you?"

"Base Ops, Stevie. I got your message and an Air Force hop to Germany and another one to here. Come get me!"

I gunned the VW the few blocks to the base runway, swooped her into my arms and kissed her, lifting her feet a foot off the tarmac. Laughing, we piled in the VW and roared back to my house. She raved about the house and Mr. Petros's garden. "Roses and orange trees! I've been living in a fifth-floor garret with pigeon shit on the windowsill and the overflowing toilet downstairs!"

"Downstairs is better than upstairs for overflowing toilets," I said.

"Right!" she laughed, throwing her bag and coat down. We jumped onto my unmade bed, bouncing, laughing, and hugging. "I was going to surprise you, I was coming on a flight tomorrow anyway! The semester's already ended."

She told me about her professors and the international crowd she'd been a part of at American University. "I really cannot believe I made the dean's list," she said. "I never worked harder in my life. It was so good to be that far away from the parents."

"Let's go for some pizza and wine," I said. "I've got a lot to tell you about *Zoo Story* and how we're improvising this poetry reading."

This night was the summit of six weeks of the most nonstop intensity I had ever experienced. There had been my car accident, dubbing the film *Seven Guns*, the Christmas party at the embassy, the *Zoo Story* roller coaster, creating the poetry reading, all while I led the double life of working at the base managing secret communications for NATO. At the neighborhood taverna, our eyes crinkling with hilarity and our laughter unchecked, we waved our hands and traced pictures in the air. How did we ever eat the pizza? Drinking the wine was no problem. Neither was flicking off the lights at home and diving into bed together.

I woke up several times that night, nestled with her. Rosebush fragrance wafted through the window and moonlight danced on the bedroom wall like a distant candle. My nose pressed against her cheek, I admired the terrain of her face an inch away in the half-light. Under her closed lids, her eyes followed something in a dream, her long lashes lacing each other, the flare of her nose and cheekbone falling away in soft focus. I thought back over my long wait to be with her, my joy at her letters, the ups and downs of our afternoon in Knossos, sharing our wits and feelings for the first time face to face. Nothing could have prepared me for this, the love and wonder surrounding us, having her alone in my bed, far from everybody, in my house in Athens. That was the final end of my virginity.

# THIRTEEN

We had no time to mourn the cancellation of our play. We threw together our poetry reading, and that Sunday night at the Hellenic American Union there was a packed auditorium. Allan led off with his guitar in the wrong key and had to start over. Sitting beside us in the fourth row, Linda clasped her hands as if in prayer and urged, "Come on, Allan!" Then he hit his stride and did a strong version of Leonard Cohen's "Suzanne," then "So Long, Marianne," then Dylan's "Blowin' in the Wind." It's an old song now, but then, in a world of assassinations and NATO trying to install nuclear missiles on Greek soil, Bob Dylan's anthem had immediate impact. Allan closed with "We Shall Overcome," most of the audience standing and joining in. I teared up.

Allan's friend Jack then read from Whitman's *Leaves of Grass*:

> *"Walt Whitman am I, a 'Kosmos' of mighty Manhattan the son,*
> *Turbulent, fleshy and sensual, eating, drinking and breeding. …*
> *Unscrew the locks from the doors!*
> *Unscrew the doors themselves from their jambs!"*

Jack stood up from his chair, leaned toward the audience and gave the peace sign:

*"I speak the password* primeval — *I give the sign of democracy!"*

The students and families applauded heartily, giving the peace sign back. The hair stood up on my arms and neck. Poetry had never seemed this real to me. Then it was my turn. I read Langston Hughes's "A Dream Deferred." My native Texas drawl and my year among Mississippi blacks colored Hughes's dark lines:

*"What happens to a dream deferred?*
*Does it dry up*
*like a raisin in the sun?*
*Or fester like a sore —*
*And then run?*
*Does it stink like rotten meat?*
*Or crust and sugar over —*
*like a syrupy sweet?*
*Maybe it just sags*
*like a heavy load.*
*Or does it explode?"*

The summer before, in '67, desperate blacks had started fiery riots in Detroit and Newark, and again in the summer of '68 in nearly all American cities after the enraging loss of Martin Luther King Jr. I felt it was right from the heart of American democracy to acknowledge our terrible faults as a nation, and I was proud to deliver the scathing words of a black poet unknown even to many Americans. Jack linked arms with Allan and me, and we waved the peace sign as the students stood and cheered. The audience was breaking the Colonels' ban on American writers by attending the event and applauding, but we didn't hear any repercussions and people said for days that they loved our performance.

After the crowd dissipated we all went over to the Hilton to celebrate our improvised triumph. I got up to look for the restroom, and a woman stopped me in the hallway. I had seen her before at a Hilton concert, but we had not talked. She was a most atypical Greek woman — tall and very thin with reddish hair, a long face and dark circles under her eyes. She was dressed in a brown-flannel long-sleeve dress buttoned up to the neck. She looked like some sort of religious fundamentalist. Standing in front of me and offering a firm handshake, she said, "You are from the poetry reading. You read Hughes, no?"

Smiling, I said yes, I'm Stephen. I asked her name. Dazed, in some inexplicable zone of incomprehension, I repeated it carefully after her. She nodded after each syllable, Ah — thee — NAHHH.

Not recognizing the name, I asked her to spell it, then asked what it meant in Greek. I was having a tone-deaf second-language moment.

She chuckled. We were leaning close to each other, our heads nearly touching, due to the noise pouring from the Dolphin Bar and the crowded lobby.

"It's the goddess! The patron saint of this city — Athéna," she said, "only we pronounce it *Ah-theen-AHH.*"

"Oh, I'm sorry," I said, feeling like an idiot and still holding the handshake. I felt the angularity of her hand. Bumpy blue veins criss-crossed them, her knuckles were chapped, her fingers cold and the nails chewed. Overall she looked ill, but her voice and the way she spoke English were clear and beguiling.

"I yam a phi-lo-lo-gy student at the University of Athens," she said, dragging the word out. "I study Faulknair, FEEjerl, your great American writers."

"Who was that one — *Fee-jerl?*"

"You know...uh," she fumbled, "we Greeks cannot say his name right. He wrote Gotsby!" she said. "Oh, my accent is horrible!"

*Gotsby*, I thought. *Oh, Gatsby!* "Fitz-ger-ald," I said, glad to have a word to explain to her. I extricated my hand and said it was good to meet her, but I had to get back to my table. Athiná turned grave, touched my arm and said, "Stephen, I want to show you something. A sculpture on the sidewalk, a bloke from Kolonaki on the north. Could you meet me tomorrow? At five o'clock? I must to talk with you. Is very important."

I said yes, a *block* north. Good, she said, sticking out her long, thin hand and firmly shaking mine again. I watched her walk away. She was so thin, she reminded me of how my mom got after the divorce. Athiná seemed fragile but at the same time formidable. I went back to the table, got Deb, and we said good-night. She needed to catch a hop to Crete to see the family early the next morning. Her mom was sick. On the way home to Glyfada, I told her about meeting this Athiná, and her odd invitation.

"Hmm. Sounds interesting. Be careful she's not CIA," said Deb.

"She's too into books. She really lit up when she mentioned Faulkner and Fitzgerald. I think she's a legit lit freak, I'm sure."

The next day, a block north of Kolonaki in the ritzy district, I found Athiná standing among a small crowd on the sidewalk looking at a white figure lying on a table. She was the tallest one there. I came up, she smiled and gestured with her eyes toward the sculpture. It represented somebody in a full-body cast. It had the blue-and-white Greek flag painted across the chest and barbed wire winding through it. Athiná took my arm and said, "We shood go." We went around the block to the square, jammed with people socializing. She chose one of the biggest cafés. We sat outside against the café wall in the shade.

"So what was that about?" I asked.

"It will be gone by tomorrow," she said. "It is by Kaniaris, one of the best Greek artists. It mocks Papadopoulos. You know heem? He is our chief dictator. He loves to say 'Greece is a patient that had to be … what is the word? Kept still, in plaster?'"

"In a cast," I said.

"Yes, so that the doctor, himself, could see how to cure it. Of course we have now been lying in plaster for two years, and the 'doctors' have no idea. We are only on a table in a cast because of them anyway. And they are making it worst."

"What about the red flowers the hands were holding?"

"Kaniaris has said they are resurrection and hope. I hope so."

A waiter brought us two waters, two little coffees, two croissants. We were at the opposite end of the square from my last visit with Allan and friends. I said to myself, *"Don't ever forget this scene. You're so lucky to be here."* Of all the lonely places I could have been sent to by the Air Force, all of the places where there wasn't much of interest off the base, I was sitting here at Kolonaki for the second time, in the heart of a famous capital city, learning about what was going through the minds of educated and interesting Greeks and their dictators.

Allan's description of how the Colonels took over flashed through my mind. "So what was the 'condition' Dr. Papadopoulos wanted to cure?" I asked Athiná.

She leaned closer. "Communism, anarchia," she said and rolled her eyes and shook her head.

Trying to get at who she was, thinking she *could possibly* be CIA or some kind of agent targeting an Air Force officer, I asked her about philology. Her face shone and she sat up. She said it was the study of languages and how they were used. Her eyes sparkled and her long hands gestured as she named the courses she took and the professors she had. She seemed authentic to me. I told her I had been in English grad classes when I was drafted.

She hailed the waiter and got some brandy to put into our coffees. "How do you say Fowk-nair?" she asked. "We don' get American speakers to teach us the pronoun-ciation."

I told her, "the way they say it in Mississippi is 'Fawknuh.'"

She tried it out: "Fock-*nuhh*." I chuckled. She laughed. "Is that how you say it?"

I gave her the usual U.S. pronunciation. "So you read about Mississippi?" I asked.

"Yes," she said, her face softening and the light staying in her brown eyes. "I love *The Sound and the Fury, As I Lie Dying, Light in Awgoost*. And I have read McMurtry, *Hood*," she said.

"It's *Hudd*," I said.

"Oh thank you. Like Huck! You see, we don' speak right. And I got a copy of *The Last Peechur Show*. These writers are companions of mine since twelve," she said. "I study the USA through these books. At least, I did, before the Colonels."

I was touched by her accent and her love for these American writers. It reminded me of the tale of the boy who dug a hole through the earth and found a friend on the other side.

"Well," I said, "those writers are great. I bet you know them better than I do. But you know, I just came from living a year in Mississippi and it's pretty bad there. It's racist. It's a fascist backwater. There are some good people, struggling, trying to be progressive there, but the government and police and most white people think the blacks are…" *How to say it so she gets it?* "They think blacks are not really modern people, and they will never be smart and must be kept down. But the white people want to keep them for their labor. Blacks are killed just trying to vote for the first time in their lives."

"What is 'backwater'?" she asked.

I said it means isolated, primitive. Her face creased into an ironic smile.

"Oh, well, sorry, Stephen, you are in a backwater here, too. My university is under attack by security police. We cannot study. There is a censor in every class." Two parties of people were settling into the tables around us. Athiná flicked her eyes at them and said she had important things to tell me but we had to be alone. I said we could go in my car and offered her a ride. She agreed, and while we cruised toward Glyfada I asked her to go ahead, tell me what she wanted to tell me.

"This car is awful for talking, Stephen," she said over the motor and wind. "Besides, we may be stopped by police." I drove by my house to show her where I lived.

"Can you take me downtown," she said. "I will find a way for us. To talk."

I drove back downtown and let her off at Syntagma Square.

"I will get a message to you, Stephen," she said as she shook my hand. I watched her walk with long strides up to the university's main building. She was fascinating. *But if she was "under attack," didn't that mean I would be, too, if I became her friend and confidant? Why did she pick me? Does she just want to tell a foreigner about the Colonels? The poetry reading! She must've taken me for a fellow English major.* I was excited to get to know this intriguing woman. I also felt myself drifting further and further from the base and my so-called military duties.

A couple of nights later, I came home after a very late session with Barker at the radio station. I saw there was a note on the door as I climbed the steps. I unlocked the door and went inside, turned on a light, and read the note, written in ornate cursive: "Midnight. Stephen,

I walked here to see you. You are not here. It is farther than I thought. I am coughing blood. I cannot wait. Athiná."

*Coughing blood? Did she come at midnight or wait until midnight? God, I don't even know where she lives or how to reach her!* Paranoia followed. I pulled the shades and curtains. I made some coffee and decided to stay up as long as I could. *What if the cops were following her?* I called Allan to ask what he thought, but nobody answered. *Of course not, idiot! It's past midnight.*

The next morning, I went into work at the base and tried to have a normal day. I didn't know how I would find Athiná and didn't want my bosses to suspect that I was involved in anything. The day passed uneventfully. That night, at home, I decided I had to find out if Athiná was having a health crisis. I called the squadron office the next morning and told Captain Al I woke up with a headache and diarrhea. "Take it easy," he said, "get your liquids, call the infirmary if you get worse. There are several guys out with that flu. You're supposed to lead the daily briefing to Colonel Fisher tomorrow. Let me know if you're not in shape to do it. I can tell Sgt. Land to do it."

"Oh, I'm sure I'll be better tomorrow, Al," I said. "But I'll let you know." I left the shades closed, left the car in the driveway as if I were still home, walked several blocks down the alley, hailed a taxi and had it drop me at Athens University, a few blocks from Kolonaki. It is a completely urban university with no campus. There was a bit of lawn but no benches, no students strolling and hanging out.

"Where's Philology? *Filologia?*" I asked an older man, who pointed up a staircase. A young woman spoke in English and directed me. I came up to a young guy at a front desk and asked if he knew Athiná, and he said, "What do you want?" I told him my name and how she and I discussed American literature, how she came to my house but appeared sick, how I needed to see if she was OK. I showed him my Air Force ID. He stared at my face for a long moment, then told me to wait right there in the corridor, holding out his hand in a "stop" gesture, and walked down the hall and around a corner. I could see into two offices from where I stood. Nobody smiled while I waited. It felt spooky. He came back in five minutes with a severe-looking young woman with oblong black glasses frames who came up very close to me and asked who I was.

"You are American?" she demanded. I told her the same story about meeting Athiná and worrying about her. She scrutinized me all over — loafer shoes, leather belt with silver buckle, my comfortable old gray cashmere crew-neck sweater, the longish hair swooping across my forehead. She asked to see my Air Force picture ID. The skin under her eyes tightened as she studied my every feature. Finally she said, "Go to the National Gardens."

I went into the National Gardens, a few blocks away on the other side of Syntagma Square. I walked down the main path about a hundred yards, found a bench in the sun and sat down. Very lush, palm trees, bougainvillea. It is the only landscaped park in Athens. I watched birds and insects. From the corner of my eye, I also watched every group of Greeks who walked by, wondering if Athiná would show up. I was anxious to learn what she wanted to tell me. All sorts of scenes from detective movies and TV suspense shows ran through my head.

"Stephen." Athiná called from behind me. I jerked around and rose from the bench. She was standing on a smaller path about ten yards away. She smiled, I smiled back and went toward her. She walked toward me with a shoulder tilted up to hold the leather strap of a heavy book bag that thumped against her hip. I took her out-stretched hand and put my other hand on her shoulder. *Don't know whether to hug her, don't know what to say.*

"How are you?" I tried.

"I yam OK. We need to walk." She took my arm and we headed farther into the park. "Stephen, I need to tell you what is going on here in Greece."

"Yes, I want to know. But why do you want to tell me?"

"The Americans support this regime," she said. "I want to tell an American what is happening here. I know you are a gentle person and love literature. I think you will be sympathy with us."

"You are kind, Athiná. Of course you are right, I don't support the Colonels and I wish my country was not supporting them. I don't want to be part of an occupying army. Your friends at the University acted scared."

"All of Greece, we are all scared, Stephen. When the Colonels staged their coup in 1967, it looked certain that George Papandreou's son, Andreas, would be elected. Andreas was educated in the U.S., at Berkeley. The Colonels say they are *suspending* freedom of speech, but we know they *banned* it. Our freedom to speak will not come back while they rule."

Athiná stood up. "We shood leave this park. We can go to Acropolis. It is always crowded, many tourists and travelers."

"But won't there be police there? There's nobody around here. Aren't we safer here?"

"We are safer *there*. The police don' wanna bother the tourist. Tourist bring money. And cameras."

We walked to the nearest street and hailed a cab. Athiná spoke to the cabbie in Greek.

"He knows me," she murmured to me. "I give tours there," she said, pointing ahead to the Acropolis. "I tell him you're another tourist."

The huge limestone mesa appeared, jutting above the center of the city. I paid the driver, and we began walking up the path up to the top from the southwest corner of the famous monument. We wound through pines and outcrops of stone to the foot of a broad stairway that switchbacked up the steepening hill. It took probably ten minutes to reach the final flight of marble steps that opened to a walkway, at least 50 yards wide. The awe-inspiring approach is huge in scale, the last 20 or so steps made of worn blocks that must have been the originals. Athiná had taken it slow, her breathing labored. There were hundreds of people from many countries along the climb, and many had stopped to rest, eating ice cream and drinking water. We entered through a portal of massive columns with buildings on either side. Athiná stopped and pointed.

"Our university entrance is copied from this portal, Stephen, you see it? It is supposed to be the entrance to eternal wisdom."

We walked some 20 yards or so through and past the grand entrance and angled to the left, past a large temple with five statues of women as its columns. It was a brilliant day. The sun's light brought out the white that was still left in the marble not darkened by the sooty patina from the pollution. Almost to the edge of the plateau, we snuggled down with our backs against a row of marble blocks. The sun's heat in them felt good on my back.

I breathed in the fragrance from the clover and thyme that was growing in the cracks between the stones we were sitting on, mixed with the freshly laundered smell from Athiná's brown dress and clean hair. To our left was the cubism of the Athens cityscape. A mile away to the east floated the higher hill of Lycabettus, three times as high as the Acropolis. With its collar of dark trees capped by a beige limestone cone, a little white monastery on the very top, it looked like a 1950s flying saucer set down among the buildings of Athens. I looked for Allan and Linda's little street on its slopes but couldn't make it out.

She began, "I have wanted to tell you what is happening here since we talk at the Hilton. I believe you are sympathetic. Eef the professor gets close to a forbidden topic, the spy raises his finger. The professor say, 'That's all for today.' And we go out. Our stoody — I'm sorry! My English is so bad. We are all stopped. If we get — if we graduate — who knows?" She said the topics forbidden in classes include democracy, freedom, crimes, politics. "We cannot talk even about Aristotélos and So-*crah*-tess."

Edward Albee was banned, so our play would have been illegal. Or at least a pretext to arrest us. Pinter. Becket. Ionesco. Sartre. Dostoyevsky. Chekhov. Mark Twain. Steinbeck. Hemingway. Tolstoy. And the three great playwrights of Greek tragedy: Sophocles, Euripides, and Aeschylus, who is known to the world now as the father of tragedy. Bobby Kennedy quoted him to the black citizens of Indianapolis, when he revealed to them that Martin Luther King Jr. had just been shot: "My favorite poet was Aeschylus. He once wrote: 'Even in our sleep, pain which cannot forget falls drop by drop upon the heart, until, in our own despair, against our will, comes wisdom through the awful grace of God.'"

Bobby's improvising of those words about King's murder rang in my memory now with double amazement — that an American politician could have brought words from Aeschylus out of his heart at a moment's notice, and that here, where the great Greek poet and playwright had walked, he was banned.

"These are the people who rule us," Athiná said.

I said, "We have had very repressive times in the U.S., too. In addition to the Kennedys and King being murdered, the FBI has helped kill or put in jail many black and Indian leaders.

"We say here," Athiná said, "when America coughs, the world gets pneumo-nía, or how you say it. But, Stephen, you passed a law to help blacks to vote. You had a big investigation of the Kennedys' deaths. The government is investigating the Chicago police. We cannot even *speak* against the police here. We have had violence in Greece like your civil rights since the *thirties*."

Then she took me into the tragedy of her family. She told me that her father was a Supreme Court judge. Two young soldiers came to their flat and kicked the door in. She cowered in a corner.

"They were country boys, draftees from Crete, I could recognize the accent. About sixteen years old. Just boys, drafted, like you. One whisper to the other, 'Which are the Communist books?' The other says, 'The thick ones.' They take all my father's law books and throw them in the — the little door, in the wall? What is it?"

"The trash?"

"It goes down a tunnel into an oven, it burns them!"

"Oh. The incinerator. How sad and stupid." *What does my country — and my "Southeast flank of NATO" military — know about this?* I shook my head back and forth, my mouth compressed into a line. *This is unspeakable.*

Athiná said we must keep moving, walking into the crowds. So we walked across the stone mesa surface, smoothed by millions of footsteps, gleaming and softly undulating. She took my arm and steered us toward the Parthenon. She began pointing up at the stone carvings along the top. She was pantomiming being an official guide. In a low voice she said that the Colonels kept the lid on this police state by employing *falanga*. "Their favorite torture, foot beating."

"How?"

"They bind your legs together, beat the bottoms of your feets with a pipe. They leave on your shoes so it don't leave no marks."

"You — you've seen this?"

"Everybody knows somebody who they tortured. The feets

swell inside the shoes. Finally, the heels and the…bottoms of the feets break down. You cannot walk normal even after weeks or months."

We climbed up the Parthenon's marble steps and crossed beneath the columns into the temple. Athiná took out a handkerchief and coughed into it. Her skin, especially on her hands, was pale, dry and flaky. I felt conflicted. I wanted to help her but I didn't want to have to help her. As I followed along, it hit me with a chill that started between my shoulder blades and spread over my shoulders. *This feeling is what I got from my mother's desolation after the divorce when I became the caretaker for her. She was wasting away and I felt pulled into her sadness and troubles.*

She pointed up at the towering columns, speaking low about torture. "They want us to know they torture. It is their way to control. The books never say this, but Greeks have always tortured, joost like the Turks. You know they ruled us for centuries? Kazantzakis writes, 'Wolves do not eat each other. But Greeks do.' The headquarters for torture is over there," she said, pointing, "by Omonia Square. The Bouboulinas Street police station, at the back of the Archaeological Museum."

I knew that word from the film *Zorba*. "My Bouboulina" was the nickname that Zorba called his old French girlfriend, Madame Hortense.

"Who is Bouboulina?" I asked.

"Bouboulina was a Greek heroine. She fought in sea battles in our war of independence against the Turks in 1820s. She was rich. She used her ships to fight the war and she herself was captain of the biggest one. She drove the Turks out of the Nafplion harbor."

It suddenly struck me: "Athiná, my commander told us not to go on that street behind the museum. He told me, 'You can hear screaming there.'"

"Of course," Athiná said, "NATO approved of the Colonels' coup."

I felt like my head was going to explode. I flashed on the Christmas party at the embassy and all the smug bigwigs drinking together. I was keeping secrets about Deborah and my activist friends in Mississippi from everybody at the base, and now I had to keep all this from my supervisors, too.

Athiná turned us toward the eastern end of the space. "We need to go, but I show you one more thing. There is where she was. The statue of Athiná. Fifteen meters tall, Stephen, can you imagine?"

My feelings of aversion at her weakness, her predicament and my urge to help her vanished, replaced by a surge of goosebumps as she made her identification with the goddess plain. She said the statue's skin was made of ivory, her clothes of gold, her eyes and face painted brightly. She was called Athiná Parthenos, meaning virgin. That's why this is called the Parthenon. She was installed here in 434 B.C. She was torn down centuries later by Christians. I'm sure my mouth was open. I was rapt, spun in the power of *hiera*, the presence of the awe of the gods.

Athiná was pulling on my arm to leave. "Now Greeks are tearing ourselves down. Someday we will awake from this."

I took her arm, so thin at the elbow. I felt totally on her side, her father's side, her fellow students' side. I felt electrified and committed, but to what? What could I do? We joined the streams of people filing down through the Propylaea gate to the traffic and pollution and police state below. I put an arm around her shoulder as we were jostled by a bunch of teens sprinting up the steps. *For those who don't know what's going on here, it's still a great vacation.* She coughed into her handkerchief, folded it quickly over the spots of red and stuffed it into her pocket. *Is it tuberculosis?* I wondered.

As we reached level ground near the street, I asked her if she wanted to stop at a taverna or restaurant. I was hungry. We had missed lunch while up on the Acropolis. I wanted to ask her so many more questions, I thought a dark restaurant would be perfect.

"Thank you, Stephen. But no. We should not be on the streets together any more today."

"But you must be hungry, too. You're weak. There's so much I need to know."

I yam OK," she smiled wanly. "I do not eat so much. I cannot."

We were nearly at the curb of the busy street. I didn't see any cops or military.

"But Athiná, what are you going to do? This is a terrible situation. What will you do?"

"I don' know, Stephen."

"Do you have friends who protect you? What about your father?"

"We all live day to day to day. My father is ill, and anyway the courts are closed. The Colonels decide everything. I go to school. I don't know what comes."

"Is there anything I can help with?"

"No, Stephen."

"Can we meet again?"

She looked up and down the street. She pressed her lips together and crossed her arms. "I will contact you if it is possible. Please, do not come for me. We are both in danger. Now I go. Please go the other way. Good-bye."

I walked away with howling feelings. *Is Athiná on their list? Were we followed? Am I being watched because I've met with her? Am I safe as an American officer? Or does that matter? That guy Ari who helped Deb and me at Sounion warned us. If I get arrested, will Captain Al and*

*Colonel Fisher intervene? And if they do, will they be so pissed at me that this is the last straw? Would they jail me? Court-martial me? Would Allan's CIA buddy Wozniak help me?*

Every bit of my Athens idyll, my dreams of Bohemian ease and the secrets of ancient Greece, had blown away.

Walking rapidly east, I was well past the Acropolis and cutting through downtown when I realized that if I kept going along this street I could go right up to Allan and Linda's. *That's it: I want to talk to Allan. My big brother. I wonder if he knows all that Athiná just told me?*

# FOURTEEN

It was a little after four as I reached Allan's apartment on Dafnomili Street. *Oh — their car isn't here. Maybe one of them is out.* I knocked on the steel gate. No answer. I pounded on it. *Where are they?*

I walked back down the street and hailed a cab to take me back home. Unlocking the door, I saw a tightly folded note had been stuffed underneath it. I went in, closed the door and read Allan's handwriting: "Steve — please come tomorrow morning, early." It was signed "Jerry." I knew that Allan really had to be in trouble to sign his note Jerry. It was the first note I'd ever gotten from him, and he never kidded about the characters we played in *Zoo Story.* I closed all the shades and curtains, left the lights on, and left the stereo playing the base radio station. I went to a taverna that had good pizza and pretended to watch a soccer game on the small TV above the bar.

That night I slept little, tossing and turning, going over and over whether I could help Athiná, or whether I should stay out of her family and university problems and burrow back into my work at the squadron, keep my job and lay low. In the morning I was dressed in civilian clothes and drinking coffee at six. I made my way across Athens to Dafnomili Street at seven. Linda let me in and we sat down at the little table. Her face was taut.

"Steve, Allan was caught and interrogated by the security police. He talked his way out of it and left on the first flight this morning for Paris."

I took in a breath and stared. My stomach flipped. "No! How did he get away?"

"He went into acting mode with them, pulled out all the stops in a fantastic story, and they let him go. He's fine now. But there's so much to tell you, why and how and what's been going on."

"Yes, tell me, I've been getting scary stories from a Greek friend, too."

"We're involved with a resistance group," Linda went on. "Allan has been wanting to tell you himself. But he worried about the Air Force — would they suspect you, arrest you, would they find out about us through you? We were so worried that they could discover the whole resistance group. But when he was caught, there was no question, we had to tell you. We didn't want to just disappear! And we need your help."

"Anything! Linda, you know how important you guys are to me!"

"I know," she said, putting out her hand over mine. "It's just so sad! He was crying when he came home a few nights ago, really late. 'Our time in Greece is over,' he said." Her eyes got shiny and she shook her head back and forth. "Our wonderful time here is over, Steve."

"Oh, God," I said. I felt incapable of putting into words how hard it was to hear this, how much I'd miss them, how overwhelming it was. "So when do you leave?"

"As soon as I can pack up our stuff. Allan's Aunt Rose and Uncle Manny are here from New York, so they can help. But we need your young strength to help me pack as much as we can into two big steamer trunks. And then — we have to ask you to do a big favor for us."

"Absolutely!" *I'll do anything for them. But I don't want to lose them!*

Just then, Rose and Manny came up the stairs and in the door. Linda introduced us, and I told them the story Athiná had just told me about the university censorship, her dad's law library, the torture. Linda's eyes widened at the bit about the law books being incinerated. But otherwise she nodded and grimaced.

"We've heard pretty much all that," she said.

Setting out sage tea and grapes and melon, she said, "Okay, I'll give you all Athens Resistance 101: how we got to this sad place."

She said there were two secret groups of organized resistance in the city. Patriotic Front was one, with about 25 people in it. It was communist-leaning. The one she and Allan were in was called Democratic Defense. It was socialist-leaning and had about 35 members. Both groups were trying to encourage the Greek public's spirits by keeping the idea of resistance viable, while never directly confronting the overwhelming firepower and brutality of the Colonels' regime. She and Allan and Jules Dassin, the Brooklyn-born film director, were the only Americans in their group. Dassin had spent a year or so in France, then came to Greece, where he directed the Greek actress Melina Mercouri in the movies *Never on Sunday* and *Phaedra,* then married her. She was a well-known leftist, who had fled to Paris immediately after the Colonels took over two years earlier.

Linda told us that she and Allan had been invited into Democratic Defense by a respected Greek writer, Vassilis Filias, who asked them to use their knowledge of English and Greek to translate the group's communiqués into English. Filias, a sweet man whose name means "kisses," among other endearments, would translate the pieces into rough English equivalence, and Allan and Linda would polish them into the proper idiom. The group then would distribute them on the streets. These constituted illegal speech and treason under the Colonels' dictates. The communiqués would attack the Colonels' suspension of civil liberties, expose their lies and paranoid fear of all things European and Western, and give news of the latest political detainees and of those tortured and exiled, as well as those released and in need of medical attention and safe recovery.

The abuses of this police state were suddenly personal, because I knew five of its victims — Allan, Linda, their baby, Niki, Athiná and her father. I listed them for Linda.

"You know more than that," she said. Remember Yannis? You met him here at our apartment for Thanksgiving, and then again when you and Allan were working on the play?"

I did remember him: slim, quiet; they told me he was a writer friend. We drank red wine and made small talk about acting.

"He was really hiding out with us," Linda said. "They had tortured him. He's an old friend, one of our dearest friends in Athens. He and his wife, Dora, have been our best friends since we've been here. He couldn't go back home and endanger Dora."

She got up and cleared off the wine glasses and little plates. "The climax of that night," she said, after Manny and Rose left the table to continue packing, "was when Allan finally arrived two hours late, sweating and coughing, from his capture and interrogation by the security police. Patriotic Front had asked him to drive a young woman to Syntagma Square so she could see if their two bombs had gone off."

*Bombs, too!* I thought.

"So the bombs had gone off, just blew out the plate glass windows in the Bank of Greece after hours, but a cop saw this woman rise up — she was supposed to stay down in the back seat — and the cop whipped out a pad and wrote their license number down. Allan saw it in the rear-view mirror and immediately knew the shit had hit the fan. He let the woman out a couple of blocks away and headed home, but they stopped him before he could get here."

"Whoa! Close call! So he didn't have anything to do with the bombs?"

"No. He said he had qualms about it because he didn't know the young woman, either, but the two groups helped each other whenever they could. So he drove our car for them."

"It had to be Allan's best acting job ever," she beamed as the story rushed out of her. "He improvised a story for the cops when they got to the main police station."

"You mean Bouboulinas?"

"Yes! Jesus Christ, that could've gone so badly! That's where Yannis was tortured. Anyway, Allan told them 'the woman in the car was a prostitute, didn't a man need a prostitute when his wife had just had their baby? Please don't tell my wife!' He hit on this line of appealing to their machismo; he flattered them, man to man. 'Didn't they understand what all us men need?' He cajoled them. 'And didn't they visit a convenient woman themselves, from time to time? So please don't tell my wife, OK?' They ended up slapping him on the back, and let him go. He told me when he got home, 'It was so strange! I was so cool, I could have lied to them for hours. It was like we were in a noir movie.'"

I was blown away that Allan and Linda had been living such a double life. It was the same feeling I'd had in Mississippi when I learned that my two buddies in officer school were under house arrest by the Air Force security goons for their antiwar activities. The fun of sea, sand, good wine and music, and late-evening talks was over too soon in both places. I was gratified that I'd picked the kind of friends both times that I loved and then came to admire for their political courage.

*But my Athens family is disappearing,* I thought, *and with my help. What am I going to face alone now?*

Linda said that the cops who took Allan in may have been duped by his performance for them that night, but Kyrio Mallios, the head torturer, always reviewed the names of anybody brought in.

"Once you go to the Bouboulinas station, you go onto the 24/7 surveillance list, and all your contacts are cataloged and scheduled for rounding up, too. And Mallios schedules you for torture." She emptied a wine bottle into our glasses. "And Steve, here's the worst part for you: Allan says they probably have your license plate number already, from photographing our house over the last few days. They may have to think twice before they pick up an American officer, but if you got picked up now, you'd be considered a part of our group."

That was scary.

She hugged me. "Let's get us all out of here. If you can come tomorrow morning, I'll have the trunks and we can pack."

I drained my glass. But I had made up my mind the second Linda asked for my help. I'd do anything for her and the baby.


At 8:30 the next morning I called the office again with tales of diarrhea and flu. Capt. Al took a deep breath and answered, "Steve. What's going on?"

"Nothing, Al. I'm just having a lot of digestive issues lately. I thought I could handle the Greek food, but..."

Al sighed. "It's been a day or two every week, Steve, for three weeks." Long pause. "Colonel Fisher's asked me about you, and I've vouched for your reliability. But your attendance and focus are not looking good. Your evaluation's coming up this month. As you know."

Al sighed and cleared his throat. "Steve, are you in trouble with a woman? Or with drugs?"

I told him no. But merely hearing Al say these things told me that my position with the Air Force had eroded to a critical point. It wasn't that I'd wanted to be a model officer; my competitive drive had stopped the day they showed us the napalm strikes in officer school. I had never considered reenlisting after my three-year assignment in Greece was up. Not in a million years would I have considered the military as a career. I had been drafted for the obscene Vietnam War, and had used the Air Force to get sent to Greece for my own education and to be near Deborah, using a bit of acting to convince the assignment people. No, as much as I personally liked Captain Al Citron, my only worry was to keep him from opening an investigation on me just as Linda needed to get out of Greece. My experience in Biloxi was that our training squadron had wasted no time in calling in the OSI — the Office of Special Investigation — to try to nail my friends Celenza and Maier, who did no more than give talks at a liberal church.

I hung up the phone and wondered how many days I had before Al had the security people put a tail on me, searched my house or brought me into his office for questioning.

The next morning, Deborah came back from babysitting her little brother and sister while her mom was bed-ridden with another mystery ailment on Crete. Deb was at the end of her rope having to play surrogate mom. "Why don't they get a paid babysitter? There are plenty of Greek girls who'd do a great job. But no, it's the eldest daughter's duty to be there. If I smell any more of that incense from those candles, I'll puke."

We took a taxi to Linda's. She had asked Rose to take baby Niki over to some friends living nearby, the French couple, Stan and Tripta

Gyr, who'd had their baby at the same time Linda had Niki. Linda greeted Deborah with a big hug. "Deborah, sweetie, so good to see you. I'm sorry you've gotten dragged into this," she said. "I haven't seen you since that poetry night, and now look at what's happened. Steve's told you the details?"

"He has. I'm so sorry you and Allan have to leave. You haven't had any peaceful time with Niki. Are you feeling OK?" Linda looked pale but insisted she was just fine.

"There are some papers I have to burn," Linda said, "and a really important box that you have to dispose of for us. I'll leave the box with Stan and Tripta, down the block, and you *must* pick it up and follow these written instructions *to the letter* tomorrow night. OK?"

She handed me a tightly rolled paper, which I stowed in my pocket. I packed most of the stuff in the living room as Linda pointed things out. Linda began to gulp air and hold a hand to her chest.

"It's okay. I'm just having tachycardia," she said. "It's rapid heartbeat. It's not my heart, it's nerves. They send my heart crazy messages."

I got up and went to her, as did Deb and Rose. Rose said, "You lie down on the couch this minute. I'm getting you some sage tea." She propped Linda up with two more pillows from the bedroom and set her tea on the coffee table. We emptied the dressers, closets and filing cabinets in big mounds. Linda helped us handle the chaos by pointing, "pack this, leave that." She said it would be better if Deborah went away from the house alone and at a different time than I did. Deb understood and gave Linda a long hug. "Give Allan our love when you get to Paris," she told Linda. To me, she said, "I'll take a taxi to the house. Be careful!" I hugged her and she went down the stairs.

"Steve, don't ever come back to this house," Linda said. She got up and came over and sat by me, putting her arms around me. She kissed me on the cheek. "Do you know that Allan thinks of you as a son? Or a brother, I mean. He told me when he left to hug you for him and thank you for all you've meant to us."

The apartment looked like a tornado had hit it, but Linda said all the important stuff had been packed. Manny had burned the incriminating copies from their mimeographed communiqués and flushed them down the toilet, cracking the bowl in the process.

I went back to my house, where I found Deborah talking to Mr. Petros's son, Kosta. He said he'd come to ask us if we would go to their family house on the island of Paros for a few days. He said his father had seen Athiná come late at night to the porch, and he'd read her note. They were worried she was being followed. We had thought we were the vulnerable ones, but now we felt embarrassed for making the Petros family vulnerable by our presence.

"Kosta, we are so sorry," I said. "Thank you for telling us. And for worrying about us. We're sorry we've endangered you."

"Of course," he said. "This is still our country and we care for our guests. But there are crazy people on both sides. The Colonels will hate you for consorting with suspicious people, and some who resist the Colonels would hate you for being in the American military. And Stephen, if they search your house — my father's house — they would come after us too."

"We can't go until tomorrow night," I said. "I have something important to do. And we have already been invited to go to the islands. Friends of my friend are going to Ios the next day. We can go with them."

"Okay. But as soon as you can, leave your car keys with me," said Kosta. "We must take your car off the streets and remove the flowers."

Deborah and I went to bed and fell instantly into exhausted sleep.

# FIFTEEN

I took on the transfer of Allen's hand-crank mimeograph
machine as if it were a truckload of guns. I was defending Allan and
Linda, and in my mind, Athiná, wherever she was, and Yannis and
Dora, wherever they were, and Deborah and me. After all the talking
and reading and listening I had done, for ten months in Biloxi and
nine months in Athens, I now had a mission that demanded physical
awareness and courage. My adrenaline surged as if my veins and
tendons had turned to copper wire.

My run from Dafnomili Street in my gray VW bug, the
mimeograph in the passenger seat, to the rendezvous point with the
Democratic Defense people — whoever they were in that do-not-look-
at-them secret exchange — was apparently invisible to the Colonels'
dragnet. But for me the twisting anonymous route on back streets
was crossing no-man's land. Whether or not my car and license plate
were already on file with the Greek police, I now identified myself
completely with the resistance. They needed all the edge they could
get as the Colonels abused the Greek people and their heritage while

the American leadership looked the other way.

Coming back into downtown I slipped into the mad traffic, glad to be flowing in a torrent of drivers who were flirting, throwing five-finger insults, honking, spewing exhaust and perfume into the night. I yelled to the empty seat beside me: "It's done!" Deb popped into my mind, alone in the house in Glyfada. *She's a trouper. She's been in the Paris riots. She won't panic if I'm late.* I longed for her company, to talk to her and sort out the collapse of our Greek adventure.

Deb had two small bags packed. A week earlier I had secured two days' leave from my squadron to accompany Allan's friends from Berkeley to the island of Ios to celebrate the successful poetry reading we'd done. With my recent days' absence, I thought Colonel Fisher might rescind the long weekend, but he didn't. He was showing patience with me, and I was grateful. After all, I had nine months of regular attendance at the office, with genial relations with people in all of our departments, before my meeting with Athiná. Now, Allan's capture changed everything for me. This trip to Ios had become more than a celebration; I needed to decide what to do now that my closest friends and advisors were gone and I might be on the Colonels' list as part of the Greek Resistance.

I left the VW at the curb by the taverna Kosta's sister owned, keys under the floor mat. Deb and I walked the roundabout way back to my house, through alleys and side streets to Vouliagmenis Boulevard north of the base entrance, and hailed a cab to Piraeus. I asked the cabbie about a cheap hotel. He gave us a thumbs up and pulled into a spot a block from the ferry wharf. He winked at me, leered at Deb. I told him to keep the change. In a second-floor room facing an alley, we pulled the curtains, locked the door, put a rolled-up towel at the base of the door, took a toke of hash and made love. We slept like stones, spooned together on the double bed. In the morning, barely gray before dawn, we ate scrambled eggs at the restaurant next door filled with guys looking grimy from long shifts on the docks or warehouses nearby. Deb and I appreciated the working-class anonymity of the port district.

We met up with Allen's friends Jack and Marlene, found the ferry going to Ios and got on. There were windows around the wide seating compartment, but sea air swirled in from open gates to the railing.

# SIXTEEN

Our ferry churned out of Piraeus heading southeast, paralleling the coast highway Deborah and I had driven when we visited Sounion, where old Aegeus threw himself into the sea when he thought his son had died fighting the minotaur on Crete. We were sailing on an ocean of fathers' grief for lost children. Deb and I felt we were lost to our fathers, too, because of the gulf between their support for the status quo and our eager pursuit of change. We called them hypocrites, but so were we — accepting the military's free ride to Greece while opposing most of what it was doing in the world. We didn't know how to reconcile that. We talked about black Americans' fifteen years of nonviolent resistance to injustice. Maybe choosing to help the Greek resistance struggle, even in a small way, was forcing our discontent into action.

The water was calm on this warming day in early May; trees and flowers were blooming all over Greece, and mares' tails graced the sky. The only gods against us were the U.S. military's nine-year co-optation of Greek theology: they had named their rockets Nike

Ajax, Nike Hercules, Nike Zeus, Atlas and Polaris, all of which were designed to carry nuclear warheads. On the other hand, they'd named their spaceships that carried astronauts — "sailors of the stars" in Greek — Mercury, Gemini and Apollo. Apollo was the god of music, poetry, plague, oracles, sun, medicine, light and knowledge, all of which were appropriate to the grand and technically brilliant effort to land American men on the moon.

A week after Deb and I took the ferry to Ios and back, Apollo 8 sailed around the moon and back in a dress rehearsal for the lunar landing. Like everybody in the Air Force, we were proud of these courageous voyagers, and like all of the United States and the parts of the world that had television, we watched with awe as the nine-year project neared its nearly inconceivable goal of walking on the moon.

Our awe was tempered, however, because we were surrounded by reminders of the Greek culture heroes and deities. Deb and I were on personal terms with Nike, or Neeka, the way the Greeks pronounce the name of their goddess of victory. We had held her in our arms. Allan and Linda had asked their friends in the resistance what to name the new baby, and they said, "Name her Neeka. We need a victory!" And so she became Niki.

We went outside to the ship's rail to watch Kea, the first island, coming into view. Though it felt as if we were leaving the mainland behind, the islands we were heading into were really the continuing peaks of the mainland mountain chains, jutting above the blue Aegean like stepping stones, one every ten or twelve miles, forming a circular group of 200 or so rocky islands that lay equidistant from Greece, Turkey, and Crete. Only twenty of them had permanent towns. The Greeks named this island world Archipelago, meaning "chief sea."

Deborah and I found two benches that faced each other on the right side of the ferry and settled into a nest of travel excitement.

Allan's friend Jack and his tall, thin girlfriend, Marlene, shared the benches with us. We barely knew them but appreciated the chance to head out to sea with in their company at that edgy moment. All I knew was that Jack had a radical background with the *Berkeley Barb* newspaper and was the guy who had passed his Brooklyn apartment along to Allan and Linda when he left New York for "Berzerkeley," as they called it.

We had water in glass bottles, yogurt in glass jars and olives in waxed-paper cones, all bought at the ferry dock from peddlers. We had maps of the islands, a battered copy of Lawrence Durrell poems, tourist guides to Ios, and a backpack each, mine already spotted with bread crumbs and a leaking carton of feta.

It was, for Jack and Marlene, just a Greek island cruise to end their visit to Athens. But for Deb and me, both amped up on adrenaline, there were uncertainties and anxieties. She was going back to the U.S. with her parents within a month, when her father's assignment to Crete was over. She had a fine semester of college credit from the American University in Paris; but although the scholarship was good for a year, she hadn't the cash to pay for a solo flight to the States. So she'd go as she came, as a member of her father's family.

How would we continue to explore our relationship? What should I do about the possibility of being linked to Allan's resistance group? If I stayed in my Air Force job and the connections to Democratic Defense became known, my Air Force bosses could endanger the lives of all those in the group and their families.

It was a big tangle of story lines, and my mind hopped from one to the other as we hopped from island to island.

* * *

As the 30-degree slopes of Kea faded behind us, and the second island, Kythnos, appeared on the horizon, I asked Deborah, "How do you feel, going back to the States with the parents?"

"The parents are being transferred back to Rantoul base, outside of Champaign, so I'll just go there and get a room in Champaign near the university. With the U of I there, and my brother, it won't be so bad. It's not Paris or Athens. The worst thing is going back to the land of giants. 'Hey, Stretch! How's the weather down there? Wanna borrow my stilts?'"

We made up dire headlines: Tourist Couple Found Floating in Sea. Man and Child Bound and Gagged off Ios. Student and Lieutenant Missing From Vacation. Bullet-Riddled Dopers Bobbing in Aegean. Commie Poets Thrown Overboard, Weighted Down with Books. American Provocateurs Dragged Behind Ferry. Bodies Thought to Be Albanian Traitors. CIA Denies Knowledge of Pair.

* * *

We napped, then read, nibbled olives and cheese, walked around the decks breathing in the sea, then napped again. There had been maybe two hundred passengers on the two decks of the boat when we started out, but clumps of them got off at each island we stopped at and now about forty of us were getting off at Ios. The ferry would proceed to the trendy tourist island of Santorini, where the rest would get off and many Europeans and Americans would get on for the trip back to Piraeus.

Jack and Marlene read and napped on their benches behind us. We talked little with them. There wasn't the same compatibility we'd had with Allan and Linda. After Kea, Kythnos and Serifos, Sifnos, the fourth island, Antiparos, the fifth (and much-larger) Paros — the second-largest of all the islands — appeared, surrounded by little boats with two men in them and sides painted orange, blue and green, with little curling-bow ornaments of wood. They all receded. We had been on the Aegean an entire day. People began to stir as Ios came into view. Deb awoke and yawned.

The ferry cut its engines and turned left into a long narrow bay that stretched about a mile into Ios. At its mouth stood a lovely whitewashed church with a dome and two towers. A few hundred yards farther, the ferry stopped at a wharf, where a long hill ran down to the sea. Greek passengers picked up their mesh bags and cheap suitcases bound with rope, the American and European trekkers their backpacks and sandals and sunglasses. It was five o'clock and the sun was still high in the west.

It took 30 minutes to climb the hill rising from the port; but at the top, the view showed the white houses of Hora, the main town, flowing down the other side and tumbling toward a crescent beach. Hora, like all the island villages, faced east or south to get the most sun in winter. The Greek builders were solar engineers long before "solar power" captured the rest of the world's imagination.

We checked into a pension with curving white walls and little decks giving access to the ocean views. As we looked over the sea, a woman called to us from the stone stairs: "Something to drink?" The sun turned the horizon gold, then orange and apricot, and finally rose and purple. Jack and Marlene joined us, and we drank lemonades and wine and watched the sunset. When it was dark, Eleni, who had brought the drinks and apparently shared her name with the majority of Greek women, brought us sheets and blankets for the bare mattress, showed us where the toilet was down the hall, and told us that cheese omelets and fresh fish would be on the dinner menu in the café.

With no lights on at Eleni's and no lights from nearby houses, the sky itself lit up our little courtyard, the village landscape, and the sea surrounding us. Never had I seen the sky gleam with such brilliant stars. They sparkled, some with flashes of green and orange. Venus shone silvery in the west, and another planet stared down with a steady ivory light — Jupiter or Saturn, I wasn't sure which. No moon this night. Down the middle of the sky ran the wide, soft glow of the Milky Way.

"I never saw more than a few stars in all the time I was in Paris. Always cloudy," Deb said.

I remembered those star books we had as kids, with the constellations superimposed on the photos of the stars in filmy drawings, all with Greek names.

"Cygnus, the swan," said Deb. "Orion. Skorpio. Uranus. The sky's Greek, all right. And part Roman, too."

I was a lover who had found his somebody to love. After we made love that night, I caressed her gently from her nape to her toes, hilly like islands above the sea. I felt so blessed. We fell asleep with air and starlight coming in through the gaps around the door.

The next day, Jack and Marlene went to one beach, and Deb

and I hitchhiked to the far southern end of Ios, to Manganari beach, about twelve miles away. We caught rides on a variety of motor scooters and little flat trailers carrying hay for sheep. Manganari was a vast semicircular bay with a golden-sand beach. There were a couple of huts and tiny booths selling refreshments, but we wanted to be alone to discuss what we should do about the police and the military situation we were in.

"You can't go back on the streets of Athens," Deb said. "If they've photographed your car in front of Allan's house, they might also have photographed *you*. And if they photographed the license plate, it wouldn't be hard for some clerk to ask a buddy working on the American base to trace it, and if they match it to you, then you'd be in weird shit with the Air Force, too."

"Right. And *you* can't go back on the streets because if they're cruising Glyfada like Kostas pointed out, you can't depend on your dad getting you out in time. The only way I see for me to stay in Athens is to take off the car's plate, take the VW somewhere remote and burn it or drive it off a cliff. Buy a new car on the base. They're changing hands all the time as people leave. And move from Mr. Petros's house to base housing. But I sure don't look forward to that!"

"Yeah, right. You'd be in Ozzie and Harriet prison on the base. Who would you hang out with? And what if Allan and Linda's group is busted and somebody knows about you? They could still come and get you and charge you with whatever they want."

"If you go back with your parents, you might not ever get back to finish up at the American University," I said.

"I know. I was doing really good there, too. But where would I get the money to live in Paris? And if I needed rescuing, Dom wouldn't be much help. He's getting madder and madder at me. I can't keep my mouth shut about Vietnam. He's got a really mean side that shows when I push him to the boiling point. He's an Italian father and I'm an outrageous daughter."

"I just hope it wasn't a mistake to tell Barker about my plan before we came to Ios. I told him I might try to get the base commander to think I'm crazy and send me back to psychiatric care in the States. I may have to go AWOL if they don't let me go. I'd have to change my name. We can go live in your grandparent's basement in Oak Park. They'll never find us in Chicago."

The next morning Deb slept in, and I was up early — the only person on the outdoor patio overlooking the Aegean. Eleni's sister made my potato omelet and café au lait. I tried to ask her for some water, but my poor Greek was something like, "Ees there *water?*" She nodded. I waited for her to go get it. She just stared at me, so I repeated my question. She waited a beat, then swept her arm out over the sea, staring at me with her eyebrows raised. I didn't get it. "Hue-morr," she prompted, breaking into a huge smile. "Hue-morr!" Ahh, yes, humor. There was indeed water! It is all around us. This is Greece. She clapped me on the shoulder, chuckling, and brought me a glass.

Before we all left the next day on the ferry back to Athens, we went to the shrine where they say Homer, the great old bard, was buried. No bones or tombstone there, but some fine souvlaki being served up by some cute island girls. We had come two more circles. Deb and I had visited the tomb of Kazantzakis, Greece's greatest modern writer, that first day I spent on Crete. Now we were at Homer's tomb maybe fifty miles away, as the dolphin swims. That evening after Jack and Marlene went to their room below ours, we had a last glass of wine and faced each other over the little round wooden table.

"I don't see any other way, Deborah," I said. "I'm leaving Greece and leaving the Air Force. Without Allan and Linda, I'll have no way to know what the Colonels are up to. I can't wait around for another shoe to drop."

"Don't blame you a bit," Deb said. "But I'll worry about you until I hear from you." She reached over and we took hands. "I hope they treat you right."

# SEVENTEEN

At dusk the next day, with a strong breeze kicking up gray waves, our long ferry ride from Ios to Santorini and back around the chain of islands to the mainland ended. We came into the Piraeus haze first, extending out over the blue water like a ceiling; then we could see the cranes and ships' masts at the port. We said good-bye to Jack and Marlene, who were going back to the States. A taxi took us to the Petros house. While Deb gathered my passport, military papers and money in an overnight case and her things in another bag, I walked down to the taverna, told them I was leaving immediately and that I loved them very much. Kostas offered to show me how they had transformed my car. "It's Greek blue now!" But I told him I had to hurry. After quick hugs I walked back to the house. I went around back and knocked at Mr. Petros's door. He came to the door looking gaunt and somber, no usual smile. I told him I had to leave that day and thanked him for renting his beautiful house to me. He asked, "My…my son talk to you?"

"Yes," I said. I thanked him for his concern and for asking Kostas to talk to me.

Mr. Petros looked pained. He struggled. "Stephen…y-you are like…your accident in car…in-in busy street. You can be killed! Danger! I know! I know them!" I understood he meant the Colonels. "Stephen, you must take *care*, for every-*thing*." I loved this sweet, elegant man, and wished I could have gotten to know him better. I shook his calloused hand with both of mine. He added his other hand to our clasp. His lack of English and mine of Greek, or his dignity, kept him from saying more. I went in the back door, told Deb the good-byes had been made, and all that remained was to psych myself up to appear mentally disturbed or drug-addled to my squadron commander on the base. "You better get going," I told her and reached to embrace her.

Then we heard someone walk up the steps and knock at the front door. A muffled voice: "Steve, it's Barker." Oh God. I opened the door and let him in. He asked if Deb and I were all right, and I told him we were about to spring my plan. Barker looked down into my face. "Steve. Look. I'm sorry, but you don't have time for your plan. You have twenty-four hours to turn yourself in to Colonel Fisher."

"What?"

Barker told us he had mulled it over, but decided it was too dangerous for me to mess with drugs off base or on base, considering what had happened to the airmen who were arrested two blocks away two weeks before. "They took those guys straight to Greek security jail, Steve, not base lockup. Could happen to you, even though you're an officer."

"What have you done?" I asked. "What the fuck have you done?!" Deb grabbed my arm and shushed me.

"So I went to the base commander. I know him socially, we've talked before."

That was perfect Craig Barker, hobnobbing with the base commander.

Barker said he told the commander that a certain lieutenant was so distraught about the situation of some of his Greek friends that he might do something drastic. He said he didn't use my name and didn't say who my friends were. He said, "The general said to just tell this lieutenant to report to his commander within twenty-four hours, and the situation would be private. But after that, he'd have to take action."

My eyes were drilling holes through his face. Barker looked down. He said that he only meant to help, that it was the best way to handle it, the least risk for me. Deb spoke up.

"Stevie, what's done is done. Craig might have made it easier for you." I took a deep breath, looked out the window and back into his face. Another angel in disguise?

"Okay. All right. Thanks, Craig. You don't need to talk to anybody else. I'll call Colonel Fisher. And please don't talk about me to anybody else!"

"All right. Sorry you're disappointed, Steve." Barker left, his mouth pressed together, eyes glaring.

Deb and I sat on the couch staring at the door after him, saying nothing for several long minutes. I fumed about Barker's commandeering of my plan.

"Well, you can't undo it now," she said. My eyes flicked around the house that had been my home in Athens.

"Sure hope Mr. Petros and Kostas stay OK," I said. "I'll never forget this amazing house. The roses. Coffee with him." Deb cuddled against me, curling her arm through mine. "As Athiná said, 'All Greece is under siege.' I hope we didn't endanger them."

"I know," Deb said. "We can leave; they can't."

Deb said she'd take the first hop in the morning to Crete. "Better I break this to my parents than have your boss do it," she said. "I'll tell Dom and Mom that you had sort of a depression because of the violence to your friends in Athens."

"Don't make Dom snoop into who they were, though."

"It's a dangerous business, this stepping outside your door," she said, quoting Frodo and using the hobbit voice we used when we read *Lord of the Rings* to each other.

"So, where's Aragorn when you need him?" I asked.

"You! You're Aragorn now! Or at least you're dubbing him, anyway!"

"Right! El Gringo dubs Old English!"


After Deborah left for Crete the next morning, I called my office at the base. I went back to the body shop and got the car from Kosta. I drove past the ball diamond and radio station, past the BX, past the maintenance buildings and parked at the 2140th Comm Squadron. When Colonel Fisher ushered me into his office, I was shaking inside and trying not to show it.

"So, Steve, I understand you have something to tell me," he said. A zing went up my spine. Since the base commander, and evidently Colonel Fisher, had been tipped off that I was the "Unstable Lieutenant," there was no reason to drum up a performance. I had lost any element of surprise. But Fisher had been warned that I was on the edge, and I still had my anger that the U.S. was supporting the Colonels no matter how brutal they were. It seemed to me the truth was my best argument. It was all I had, anyway.

"Well, sir, I didn't realize how serious you were when you said we should avoid Bouboulinas Street. There *is* screaming there, like you warned us. Do you know who they torture there, Colonel?"

His eyes tightened. "I assume it's criminals, Steve. That's who the police have to deal with. We're in a part of the world that doesn't agree with our standards of custody and interrogation. What seems extreme to us is normal in this part of the world."

"So would you consider the most famous composer in Greece a common criminal in need of beating? Would you consider a university philologist a criminal in need of torture? Or a Supreme court justice's law books being dangerous communist books?" I paused for a second or two, but his eyes didn't lose their impersonal coolness.

"Steve, none of us have access to internal Greek affairs. We have to assume that if the police are having difficulty keeping people within the bounds, and that would include not helping the communists, that it's their business. We don't interfere in Greece's internal affairs."

That was such an absurd, disingenuous statement I wished I could've laughed in his face. "But Sir, we use half of their airport! We broadcast our music to their people against their government's wishes! We wanted to put nuclear missiles on their land! NATO approved the friggin' coup and gave the Colonels a blueprint to carry it out and named it for one of their ancient heroes!"

"Steve, there are international strategic considerations here, not just what the Greek people want."

"Sir, I protest that you would warn us not to go where there's screaming but not care to investigate what they're doing there." I poured out my frustrations at the Colonels and how they were abusing decent people, including people I knew well. I didn't name anyone. I raved about the sickness of NATO's support of dictatorships. I told him it was tearing me up so much that I could not see doing my job, being part of that machine. He looked at me with a kind expression.

"Steve, a lot of what you're saying is beyond your ability or my ability to affect. It's for the higher-ups to consider. We're out here on the fringe of everything. Let's just treat your situation as a medical matter, not a police matter."

A rush of relief came on me when he said "medical, not police" because that meant I would not be interrogated, jailed or court-martialed for dereliction of duty or whatever they might have cooked up. "Medical" meant mental health. It meant psychologists and psychiatrists. It meant no investigation into what Athenians I knew or investigations into the Resistance.

The colonel went on, "If you'd report to the base infirmary by six tonight, they'll take care of you. There's a Dr. Edwards there and he'll be expecting you." He stood up and came around the desk, offering his hand. "It's been good having you work with us, Steve. Don't worry about your house or any of your things. We'll get them to you. And I want to wish you good luck in the coming year. I hope you can be at peace about whatever's troubling you."

*"Whatever's troubling me?" I just told him. But I guess denial and silence are his best protection, too.*

I drove back to my house. Without Deb to greet me and with Mr. Petros not in his apartment, it seemed like an abandoned house of a past life. I took my stash of hashish, unwrapped the foil around it, and buried it under the rose bushes. *Go back to the earth and give these old roses a long buzz while you're at it,* I thought. I packed a small suitcase with my dark-blue long-sleeved uniform shirt and pants, my shaving stuff, toothbrush, deodorant, aspirin and a change of socks and under-wear, in case I had to stay over at the base hospital. I looked around at the white walls, and for the first time I could remember, I put my hands together in praying position and spoke aloud my prayer that Allan, Linda, Mr. Petros, Deborah, Athiná, Kostas, and I be blessed, safe and relieved of the Colonels' menace. I shut the front door, left the key under the mat and drove back to the base to meet my medical angel.

When I met Dr. Edwards, I felt cool and collected, and he seemed kind and empathic. But when he began to ask what had been bothering me, I decided to take this chance to put my view of the Greek travesty on the record, rather than get his pity or respect. Whatever a "medical solution" to my dilemma might be, I wanted him to know that this interview was the first step in my separation from the Air Force, not a negotiation that might result in my getting sedated and held for a few days or weeks until I was "better."

He looked to be about twenty-eight, a recent med-school grad drafted, like me, into the service. His twin silver captain's bars were pinned to the lapels of a long white doc's coat, which he wore over a pale-blue uniform shirt and navy-blue tie. He was expecting me, he said, and closed the door to his small office behind us. I vented my rage and grief again, demanding to know if he knew about "not passing by the Bouboulinas Street torture place" and how the university was shut down by right-wing censors. I thought I might have a chance to play on his physician's aversion to brutality. He blinked. He was writing things down as I vented. He looked up at me steadily and apologetically when I came to the end of my testimony.

"Look," he said, "I'm just a general practitioner. I really don't know anything about … mental or emotional things such as you're describing, or about Greek politics. I'm going to have to refer you to the Air Force hospital at Ankara, Turkey. They have a psychologist there who might be of more help to you than I can be. You'll have to stay here tonight — we have a private wardroom with a bed you can use. The flight will leave at nine tomorrow morning."

The next morning, they flew me to Ankara, where the U.S. had a larger base. Ankara was the seat of Turkey's government, out on the high desert a third of the way into the oblong country. Turkey was tied to Greece because each had ruled the other over the centuries, and they had deeply influenced each other, which was obvious in their food and architecture. As we flew over the western third of the country, it looked from the plane that there were ruins everywhere.

The cab I took from the airport to the American base was a classic 1953 Chevrolet, just like the one my childhood buddy's family had in the Oak Cliff side of Dallas when we were ten and twelve. The driver was delighted to have an American history nerd to educate on the glories of his city and nation.

In fifteen minutes, as we wound around a rocky hill topped with the remains of a castle, the cabbie had hipped me to the fact that Ankara's old name was Angora, that they had given the world the long fine mohair wool of Angora sheep, the silkier wool of Angora rabbits, muscat grapes, Turkish coffee, and pears and honey to boot. As we bounced along bad roads, without missing a beat he pointed out Hittite, Phrygian, Hellenistic, Roman, Byzantine and Ottoman Empire ruins.

The psychological clinic at the U.S. base abruptly brought me back to the Cold War between the command structure and the draftees and hapless guys like me who weren't having a good time carrying out the New World Order. The psych clinic had a waiting room and a day lounge, separated by glass. As I sat in the waiting room, I saw that three black soldiers were playing a drugged version of chess. One guy was claiming to have checkmated his opponent, and the two other guys were loudly disputing the move. The first guy theatrically replayed the move for them, punctuating each step with a vocal "Boom! Boom! Boom! Checkmate, brothas."

The door of the doc's office opened, and a white-coated guy, similar to the Athens base doc, came out. "Hi, I'm Dr. Henderson," he said to me, holding out his hand. "Come on into my office. Their game," he smiled, nodding at the players, "is getting a little influenced by the phenobarbital."

*Hmm. So that's the sedation of the moment.*

He looked over my file. "Why don't you tell me why they've sent you here," he said.

I took a deep breath and told him the same stuff I'd told Colonel Bert and Dr. Henderson. Just as in Athens, I started off smoothly, but during the telling my emotions boiled out of their hiding places. My "intake statement" turned into a jumbled recap of all the violence and stupidity I'd seen since JFK had been killed in my home town, and the losses of the male leaders I'd admired, beginning with my dad and continuing on through Medgar Evers, Martin Luther King, Bobby Kennedy, my radical buddies in Biloxi, and ending with Allan Wenger and Mikis Theodorakis. By the time I got to the Athens situation, I was pretty emphatically amped up. I told him clearly about NATO's blessing of the Colonels' coup and their reign of torturing, and the people I'd met who testified to those situations.

Dr. Henderson continued writing in my file for a couple of minutes. Then in a kind voice he suggested, "Let's see. Maybe it would be a good idea, right now, for you to let the Air Force be your father. You mentioned in your intake statement just now that you missed him. Don't you think, Stephen — if I may call you Stephen? — that right now, one of the best things we can do, is to get you a little structure, a little, um, comfort, against these things that are bothering you so much? One of the best ways available to us, right now, would be seeing the Air Force not as your literal father, I know he's really caring for you now, wherever he is, but as what we might see as your support system, your father in that sense. I know your commanders and peers at the Athens squadron think highly of you. They're worried about you. And they could be this sort of net for you, an extended father, so to speak, like a village. Could you let that comfort you?"

"No, that wouldn't work for me, Doc."

"You know," Dr. Henderson replied, "it seems when things build up and build up, we can sure use some shoulders to lean on. And — "

*"Jesus Christ!* Is that all you care about, just keeping calm?! None of you *care* what our American money is *doing?* And who's getting killed in the *process?"*

"Well, Stephen," Dr. Henderson began, his head looking down, "it is, in reality, a dangerous world. Right here where we're sitting," he raised his eyes to mine, "we are, in reality, surrounded by communist countries and communist sympathizers. And Islamic societies. We can't do anything about that. Our leaders have to address that. We can support each other, medically and health-wise, as best we can. Which is what I meant by my suggestion about fathering. It's all I can think of."

"Does nobody in this Air Force culture have any ethics? Any human feelings? Any thoughts about *right and wrong?"*

"Well, Stephen, those are questions that philosophers have argued about for many centuries. I'm sure that in Athens you heard of Socrates and Aristotle. Coming to an agreement on things of ethics wasn't easy for them, either."

"Did you know that reading them or talking about them is now banned in Greece?"

He sighed. "I'll have to forward your paperwork to Sheppard Air Base in Texas, where they have a psychiatrist. You'll leave here on a flight tomorrow afternoon."

I had tried to shape this interview and thought I'd failed. But as I walked back to the dorm room they'd provided me to pack for the next leg of my odyssey, I realized I'd actually succeeded. They were sending me back to the States.

My flight to the U.S. was in a giant C-140 cargo plane that had rows of
seats bolted to the fore part of the cargo bay. It was called a "Starlifter."
In this drafty flying barn, I met my first Vietnam evacuees — a row
of guys with bleary eyes, wrapped in bandages and dressed in hospital
pajamas, who said they were on their second lap around the world —
they'd been put on the wrong planes twice. They didn't know why.

We landed in Wiesbaden Air Base in Germany and stayed
overnight. The next day I was on a flight to the U.S. Upon landing
in Chicago, I was immediately transferred to a plane that dropped me
in Wichita Falls, Texas, on July 4th, 1969. If I'd had some firecrackers,
I would've been lighting up the sky celebrating my escape from the
military.

At Wichita Falls, the afternoon temperature soared over a hundred
and eight degrees the first week I was there. Tar on the streets and
sidewalks of Sheppard Air Force Base melted and made big translu-
cent bubbles. The base sprawled on the upper Texas plains just where
the prairie started to buckle into arroyos and escarpments. The west
begins here. Ironically, it was the closest base to my Dallas home. It
was disorienting to find myself in a mental ward 140 miles from the
place I'd escaped from three years before with such passion and
idealism and hope, and now to be sitting on vinyl furniture in a rec
room watching my fellow inmates sit in group therapy sessions, their
legs spread wide, their hands clasped over their crotches, their eyes
wary. Our mental ward was one of five floors in a whole psychiatric
wing here at Sheppard. I could only imagine how surreal it must be for
guys coming back from combat in Vietnam.

July 4th was a day off for the psychiatrist I was assigned to. I
had two days to get my bearings and psych myself up for my final
mental-health interview. I was the only officer patient there among

dozens of enlisted guys. Arrayed in a circle in the group-therapy sessions was a whole spectrum of worn-out, broken-down and furtive men. The ones most poignant to me were clones of Sgt. Long and Sgt. Bobby Land from back in Athens — forty-something men with deep shadows under their eyes, alcohol-red noses and the pockets of their robes full of green Librium and orange Valium pills. Guys would look at me and offer, "Which ones you want? I got both," holding out a handful of pills.

Finally my doctor was back. I had ratcheted up my anxiety, because if he didn't believe that I didn't belong in the service, there was no option after him. For the two hours after breakfast on the day of my midmorning appointment, I sat on a sofa against the north windows of the rec room, staring straight ahead, rubbing my palms up and down along my thighs, going over my intake interview. When they called my name, I was wound tight.

They put me in a small interview room alone. I heard footsteps approaching the other closed door — clack, clack, clack, clack. I held my breath, hearing my heart thump. When the door opened and a doctor stood there, a good half of my tension just atomized into the air. He was wearing a white coat and captain's bars, all right, just like Edwards and Henderson before him, but his brown curly hair was tousled and on his face there was a three- or four-day growth of beard. And sticking out of the bottom of his white coat were bell bottoms! Striped! And penny loafers with no socks!

"Hi," he said, "I'm Dr. MacDonald. Tell me what's goin' on."

Despite the clues that he was a cool guy, I sucked a deep breath and marshaled all the evidence I had lived through. I gave him the whole speech I had given Henderson, toned down a bit, plus more of the details Athiná and Allan had given me. I threw in being a grad student and counting the bullet holes on Guadalupe Street. By the time I was done I was rocking back and forth and rubbing my hands on my thighs like someone having a real anxiety attack. Which I was. Which of course he saw.

"Okay, Steve," he said.

He paused, and I couldn't believe what he said next.

"Don't worry. I'll get you out. But it'll take six weeks. I have to write it up in a plausible manner. Have to do a report observing you here in group therapy. So relax. There's light at the end of your tunnel."

Air streamed back into the room until euphoria bloomed in my lungs. "Oh God. Thank you, Doc! *Thank you!*" I wanted to hug him, but he was writing in my file, which was now an official-looking medical chart. "Are you a regular Air Force doc?" I asked before I left.

"No. I was drafted, like you. Actually, I registered at the end of college at UCLA as a conscientious objector. But they kept after me. I got a lawyer who negotiated a deal with them: as soon as I graduated medical school, they'd draft me to serve as a psychiatrist. I don't know how much freedom of the base you'll have, but I'm in the wood shop all the time when I'm not here. If you like woodworking maybe you could come over there. If you see a little red Alfa Romeo, that's my car." His name tag showed that his first name was Allan, which I found to be reassuringly significant. An angel named Allan in an Alfa! My military journey ended with another kind man easing my transition. I had consistently been provided with decent and helpful men at every crossroads I came to. That was worth celebrating, and restored my faith in life.

"One more thing, Steve. There's a call you have to make," said Dr. MacDonald. "I was required by regulation to call your parents because you'd been released by your assignment in Athens and brought to this psychiatric ward. I explained to your mother that we might have to keep you for observation, but that I thought your file indicated that you weren't really mentally ill. So call her when you can to reassure her. Tell her that it will take about six weeks to observe you so I can write up your discharge paperwork. In between talks with me, you'll be free to go anywhere on base or in Wichita Falls. We might even get you passes to go out of town in a couple of weeks."

I called her before I left the ward. She was distraught and worried. She didn't seem to believe anything I said about the situation in Greece. I told her I liked my doctor and would be in touch soon. I was in no mood to talk to any more people who didn't believe what I said about the Greece I had just experienced. I didn't want my mom or my dad hovering around and peering at me to see if I was really mentally OK.

I had to keep myself from skipping and laughing out loud as I crossed the day ward and went down the stairs and out into the muggy air; but outside, I skipped and *Wahooed!* I walked and walked around the hospital and a sandy playground next to it, replaying the last week in my head and thinking about Deborah in Illinois. I didn't have to look over my shoulder anymore. I was going to be free to go to Champaign again and be with her.

# EIGHTEEN

For the next six weeks, I was assigned to a minimum-security duplex apartment near the hospital complex on base. This entire six weeks was dominated by the 24/7 back-to-back playing of *Sergeant Pepper's Lonely Hearts Club Band*. Someone in an adjoining duplex played it, turned it over and played the other side, over and over and over. I came to know every note, every word, every chord. It wasn't a bad deal; it could've been Creedence Clearwater or Percy Sledge or Iron Butterfly — *In-A-Gadda-Da-Vida* — all day and all night. But *Sergeant Pepper* was filled with such good writing and different textures of music. I agreed with Paul and John that we needed to sit back and enjoy the show, we needed to get by with a little help from our friends, we needed to float with Lucy in the Sky. I totally understood when I learned, years later, that Leakey's team in the Rift Valley of Africa named their find of the oldest upright hominid Lucy, because they had been listening to *Sgt. Pepper* when they found her three-million-year-old bones.

A lot about life in the past three years, from Austin to Mississippi to Athens and back to Texas, made the lyrics of "A Day in the Life" sound … well … like my life.

My roommate was André, a tall, lanky and energetic black guy who, like me, had had enough of the Air Force — he, because of bigots who sabotaged his desire to stay in twenty years and retire with benefits; me, because I couldn't risk letting the kind and friendly gentlemen I worked with find out about the Greek resistance through me.

"I'm gay, obviously," André told me as we sat talking and smoking a joint we got on the base black market, "but I never used it to stay out of the service," he said, leaning forward, his elbows on his knees, sitting on the side of his bed. "I wanted a career, you know, money and travel too. My dad and uncles were Army guys. I wanted to stay in. I kept bein' gay to myself — I woulda stayed in until I could retire. But it didn't work out that way. I ran into some ignorant, cruel fuckers. There was nobody I could appeal to because my supervisor was one of 'em, and they fucked up my personnel file. So I'm usin' the gay thing now! Let this homo *out*, baby!"

André also had one record album and a cheap box to play it on. It was Chicago's first album, *Chicago Transit Authority*. André took exquisite delight in playing the cut, "Does Anybody Really Know What Time It Is?"

"Well?" he'd ask. "Does anybody?" He'd cackle, slap his knees, slap handshakes with me. "Nobody around here knows but you and me!"

I got my official diagnosis from Dr. Allan MacDonald on August 19, 1969, the day after my 25th birthday. My medical file read that the Air Force psychiatric hospital considered me to be having a psychotic reaction to the stresses of my job, expressed as schizoid depression brought on by my service in Greece. They declared me ten percent disabled. They were giving me an honorable medical discharge and paying me the two and a half months pay I'd never received while under observation and en route from Athens to Ankara to here, plus the proceeds from the "yard sale" my squadron had held for my books and record albums, stereo, big speakers and TV. The base police had traced my car and added it to the yard sale. They also must have added some sort of severance payment since the diagnosis said my condition was *caused by the Air Force*. So I was leaving the employ of Uncle Sam's Cold War Empire with a lump sum of about $8,000. I ran all the way back to the duplex and told André. "Brother Gay! I'm getting out! I'm ten percent schizoid!" I hollered.

"Well, right *on*, boy!" He hugged me, we swung around, he rubbed the hair on my head. "Way to *go*, brotha! Yes, yes, *yes!* But ten *percent?* You're only maybe eight at the most, Stephen! No ten, no *way!*" He dug out the roach from our joint and lit it up. We took turns deeply inhaling what was left of it. "This is fabulous! I'm so glad for you, Stevie. You go on out there now, and tell people what time it *is*, mojo! Now wish *this* homo luck on *my* diagnosis!"

The world kept putting more great guys in my path. This small, crucial irony was very apparent to André and me. The most interesting people we met preferred the psych ward to the medal ceremony, or at least knew when to bend the law and get out of town when the sane people started acting crazy.

I had to wait around a week for the personnel office to process my discharge and cut my checks, but it was lovely to spend time with André and see him get a similar medical discharge to mine. We took several fellow mental patients whom we had met at the sandy playground out for a lavish dinner at a Mexican restaurant a block from the base. Two of these guys had raided a doc's trash can and came up with a memo from the Secretary of the Air Force telling Sheppard that the Air Force was getting a sharply rising number of people claiming various odd ailments and religious objections to the war. The memo said that having the psychiatric unit process people out with due diligence in describing their psychiatric conditions was cheaper for the Air Force than having the legal people fight their complaints in the Judge Advocate General's system.

I caught the civilian two-engine commuter plane from Wichita Falls to Dallas to check in with my mom to reassure her I wasn't crazy. Unfortunately, our trajectories were so divergent that we could hardly converse. She was frightened that I'd gotten a psychological discharge. She couldn't appreciate that it was a medical discharge and an honorable one. She seemed to think it was a failure on my part.

"I don't know how I'll tell all our friends who knew you in high school about this," she said. "Everybody expected you to do so well."

A fellow teacher of hers who knew me when I was in high school came over for dinner. I explained that Greece had been a police state supported by the U.S.

"My Lord," this woman said. "That's never been on the news. Did you really know people who'd been tortured?"

I didn't want to give her names, dates and places, in case Deborah's dad was tracking us.

Mom said, "Well, we have a Greek vice president, Spiro Agnew. He was governor of Maryland, where I went to college, you know. You'd think we would have heard about this."

"Well. I'm truly surprised you haven't. Europe is about to kick Greece out of the Council of Europe for torturing and imprisoning anybody who opposes them."

Over hot chocolate before bed, she looked at me with deep sadness.

"Are you really all right, my son?"

"I am, Mom. I really am. But I've changed. I don't see anything the same as before."

"But you had to see a psychiatrist."

"I wish more people could see one. Especially the people running our government and supporting the dictators in Greece. It was so much better, Mom, than being investigated by *our* security police. That could have endangered my Greek friends."

"Oh my Lord. I just don't understand."

My mother and father had both remarried. My dad had moved from Dallas after the divorce and now lived outside Austin. Both of their new spouses were Nixon fans and had little interest in what Greece was like. Mom's new husband was fifteen years older than she was, drove a Cadillac, and just wanted to go to dance parties and sip highballs. Ironically, I had pushed my mom into his circle by giving her name to a computer dating service for seniors when I had left her apartment to attend graduate school in Austin. I paid the $100 fee the day before I left town, because she suffered so much isolation and never had a chance to meet men. Computer dating was in its infancy, but she soon found Al and they married.

The updated, but same old, furnishings and wall decorations; the faith in and admiration for Nixon; the suffocating comfortableness of her life drove me to leave for Champaign after three days.

I took a flight to Chicago and a commuter plane down to Champaign in mid-September, looking down at the cornfields and the highway traffic I'd hitchhiked through when I came here to see Jim. I got pleasant tingles thinking of my first two angels down there below, the recruiting coordinator and Deborah. I had written Sgt. Cuomo from my hospital ward to ask how to reach Deborah, and he had delegated that task to Jim, who called my mom to give her the address where Deb was subletting a basement apartment from a guy who baked artisan breads, studied Renaissance music, wore a cape and now lived for free in some steam-tunnel grotto beneath the University.

I was euphoric as the cab let me out at her address. The setting was American Gothic, a large two-story house with dying elm trees in the yard. I went down the outside steps to the basement door, which was worn and had dry vine tendrils looping across, attached to the screen with tiny feet like dried starfish. Deborah peeked around the door when I knocked. She looked very small and unsure. "It's you," she said.

"Yup, it's me. What's wrong? Are you in shock?"

"Aren't you?" she asked.

"Of course I am."

"Well. Come on in," she said after a silent pause during which I could hear the oak and elm leaves rustling in the wind and hear my heart banging in my chest. I felt fear rising that something was going to be wrong or very difficult in our adjusting together here in Champaign. Deb stepped back so I could enter. I wanted to sweep her up, but we both seemed so out of context, so lost.

"Wow," I said as I took my coat off and leaned against a brick wall painted white. "I've been imagining us running together into each other's arms," I said.

"I'm not feeling much like a Hollywood movie," Deb said. "So are we going to live together now? I don't know why, but … it seems weird." Of course it felt weird. We had been together all of three weeks, spread over two years and thousands of miles. All the rest of our conversation had been in letters. I hadn't considered that; I had just run as fast as I could from the military toward my best friend, the only person in the world who could understand what I'd been through. Neither of us had ever lived with anybody of the opposite sex. I was naïve and codependent, as the condition came to be named years later. I didn't know where else to go. Plus, I was still in love with her.

We took small steps toward each other, touching and folding slowly into each other, just standing there with flashbacks of our shared memories.

"I don't know what I want," Deb said, looking up with her hands on my chest. "Or what I'm doing here." Then she took me by the hand and said, "Well, I'll give you the tour."

There was a tiny windowless living room with orange shag carpet and two funky sofas facing each other with barely room for legs in between. A metal shower stall the size of a phone booth stood against one wall beside the kitchen, with no dish for the soap. The toilet was in a broom closet. That *really* felt underground to me. Maybe I wanted a bunker to meditate in, or to defend if they tried to draft me again: "Cheater! Your country still needs you!" The kitchen was like a ship's galley — reach to the right, there's the dish drainer, stick out your left arm, that's the end of the two-burner stove.

"Over here's the bedroom," she said, "and as you can see, it's bigger than the living room." Pale gray light filtered through two ground-level windows. It was dingy. Depressing. We sat on the edge of the bed, then lay down in our clothes, turned toward each other on our sides, and stared at each other silently.

I raised up on my elbow, and felt my elbow sink in as the mattresses slipped apart. "Yeah," she said, "watch out for the crack." The queen-size bed was two twin beds lashed together by the inside legs. The sheets, blanket and bedspread covered the crack between them, but they weren't solid. We would have fun with this metaphor in the coming days, laughing about the fault line. But still, there it was, between us. The Crack. We got up and sat at the tiny table in the kitchen.

Deb fiddled with her hair. "So congratulations, Stevie. They let you go with no strings?"

"They did. I met another angel named Allan, my shrink. I got about eight grand in back pay. And I can apply for disability."

"For what?"

"They diagnosed me ten percent schizophrenic," I said with a straight face.

"Ten percent schizophrenic!" Her face relaxed, her teeth showed in a grin and she shone with her customary light for the first time. "Ten percent! How do they measure *that?!*" she cackled, nearly tipping her chair all the way over.

"Don't ask me. I'm mentally disabled!"

Deborah came to life, trying to parse my ten percent schizoid diagnosis.

I brought up all the craziness she'd been through with her security-service dad and the riots in the Paris revolution. "I bet you're eleven percent yourself!"

"I'm at least that!" she cried. "You get five just for being short! And two for being Italian! Two more for being a book head! And at least two more for testing all the hash of Europe! Oh — and four more for being female!"

"You know," I said, "I've noticed in our group therapy sessions that you may be pushing *sixteen* percent."

"I'm schizoid and I'm proud!" she said. "Hey, remember that Mateus wine we drank at Allan's? They have it here, too." She pulled a half-full bottle from an orange-crate shelf and poured us two jelly jars full. Finally, we began to relax.

"Have you heard from Allan and Linda?" she asked.

"Yeah, they're fine. They stayed with Yannis and Dora the first two weeks in Paris. Tiny apartment on St. Germaine, right near where your coffee shop was. Get this: the first day they went out walking, they ran into Jules Dassin and Melina Mercouri. Isn't that wild? What a small world! They even shared an apartment with them for a while."

I told her how Allan also ran into one of his former students from Athens College one day, on the Champs Elysée. The guy told him that right after he and Linda left Athens, they arrested Allan's whole resistance group and put them on trial. The judge noted that there were supposed to be two Americans in the group, Allan and Mr. Dassin, both Jews. He said that the two Jews must have fled Athens for money. He said to the courtroom, "Can you imagine Jews not running after money?" The student didn't know what their sentence was.

We sipped our Mateus and rolled our eyes at the xenophobia oozing out of the Greek regime.

We were geographically discomfited by the unbounded vastness of the prairie surrounding Champaign and the size of the University of Illinois campus, with its grid pattern of streets and immense brick buildings with open space between them, such a reversal of Greece's mountains, vertical island silhouettes and narrow, twisty village streets. It took weeks for us to adapt to our spatial disorientation. The University did have some refuges from the monotony of the plains: photography exhibits, bars, hamburger joints. After I had stayed at Deb's place for about a week, she said one night, "I guess you should really stay here with me. We're the only people who understand each other."

"I agree. We'll have to try not to drive each other crazy."

Living together was a reassuring grounding for us. We had a loved one to come home to.

Soon we gained entry into circles of new friends through Deb's brother Jim. He was producing an original musical; Deborah auditioned and got the lead role. He produced another "happening," as they were calling events staged either in unusual venues or with loose structure. It was presented as a mock discovery of a strange creature called a Mormo. Deborah wore a head-to-toe suit with batwings, and was held prisoner in a slow-moving pickup truck.

Jim had also written songs for a band he put together called "The Spoils of War." He booked a day of recording time at a studio about an hour from Champaign and asked me to sing the lead on a rock tune, "Ring, Magic Telephone, Ring". Jim got me a part-time job at the local outlet of the national chain Discount Records, so I was plugged back into the music world. Ten cartons would arrive on a UPS truck with 500 copies of the new album *Crosby, Stills and Nash* (the one with "Marrakesh Express" on it). Another 500 would arrive the next week as the album spread through the youth culture. Bob Dylan's former road band, The Hawks, put out an album of their own called *The Band*, with such a stark sepia portrait of the five members in the Woodstock, New York, woods in their motley winter clothes and beards that people felt it was channeled from the 1920s or even the 1870s when their songs "The Weight" and "The Night They Drove Old Dixie Down" played. When the store manager found out I had been in radio, he gave me the store-sponsored night jazz show on WILL-FM, the campus station, where I became immersed in Miles Davis and Cannonball Adderley (if only Barker knew.) It was a far richer musical education than the one I'd started at LBJ's station three and a half years before.

But though these ventures were interesting and fun, none of them satisfied Deb and me. For her, it was a step backward into being Jim's little sister again, with him as creative impresario and her as performer of odd characters. As the weather turned mostly gray and the snow started lingering on the sidewalks and trees, we went looking for our own opportunities and recorded improvisational promo spots for events at the university. We moved out of the basement apartment and into a second-story room in an old frame Victorian house on a corner of Wright Street. It had a claw-foot tub, and the kitchen was a little bigger than the one in the basement apartment. The floor slanted toward the far outside corner of the all-purpose main room. We could have friends over and say, "Watch —" Then we'd drop a jack ball and it would roll diagonally across the room, like in an Ernie Kovacs illusion.

As in Greece and Paris, there was a violent, menacing current running through Illinois. The year before we had returned to the States, we'd read how the Chicago police created the most horrific scenes ever witnessed at a political nominating convention in U.S. history. The Democrats had assembled in Chicago, 150 miles north of Champaign, with their party bitterly split between the establishment candidate, Hubert Humphrey, and Eugene McCarthy, who had become leader of the furious antiwar, antiracism coalition of many groups. President Johnson had already announced he would not seek reelection because of the power of the antiwar movement.

The violence started on Wednesday, August 28, 1968, when a rally in Chicago's huge Grant Park was attended by about 15,000 protesters, many in the dissident uniform of bell-bottomed jeans, long hair, headbands, beards, and Army Surplus jackets; but thousands of average college kids and longtime peace activists also showed up, because they smelled a disaster coming. The police moved in with billy clubs and tear gas, clearing the park and leaving only a small circle of devotees around Allen Ginsburg, the famous Beat poet, who was chanting *Om* to defuse the violence. But the police and demonstrators went on into five days and nights of protests, marches, clubbings, tear-gas attacks, and arrests, culminating in dozens of journalists, cameramen and innocent bystanders being trampled and beaten in the city street in front of the hotel that was the Democratic Party headquarters. Convention delegates watched in horror as their convention turned into a police riot.

By the time Deb and I arrived in Champaign, the feds had indicted eight antiwar protest leaders: Abbie Hoffman and Jerry Rubin of the "Yippies" party; Bobby Seale, a Black Panther Party leader; 54-year-old David Dellinger, chair of the National Mobilization to End the War, who looked "like an off-duty Scoutmaster" according to one journalist; Rennie Davis, national director of Students for a Democratic Society (SDS), an Oberlin grad and U of I graduate student; Tom Hayden, co-founder of SDS; and two quiet, detached men, John Froines and Lee Weiner, both chemists indicted for making stink bombs. The police called the stink bombs "incendiary devices."

The trial began in Chicago Federal District Court on September 24, 1969; early in October I was given a leave of absence from Discount Records so I could write an account of the proceedings for *WIN* magazine, which stood for Workshop in Nonviolence. *WIN* was the main outreach tool for the War Resisters League in New York, founded back in the 1920s.

On October 9, Judge Julius Hoffman called in the National Guard to control the crowds that grew outside the courthouse. It was a national circus of a trial, so crowded that Deb and I could not get into the federal building, let alone the courtroom. We had just heard Fred Hampton, head of the Black Panther Party of Illinois, speak to a huge rally in front of the fifty-foot-tall Picasso sculpture in Daley Plaza. Hampton told the crowd, "Judge Hoffman, now, the man so old and wrinkled, he have to *screw his hat on*." And he got on a roll with insults like, "The leaders of this country so stupid," he said through his own laughter, "they throw the candy bar away and *eat the wrapper!*" The crowd roared at this bold, funny new black organizer, only 25 years old. But of course the police were not amused, and on December 4th, Chicago police fired 200 bullets into a West Side apartment at dawn, killing Hampton and his Panther brother Mark Clark while they slept. *Two hundred bullets, while they slept.* It was another in a long line of political assassinations of black organizers.

The other Black Panther in the trial spotlight, Bobby Seale, demanded to represent himself; the judge refused. Seale called him a racist pig and fascist dog. The judge ordered Seale bound to his chair and gagged. When artists' sketches of Seale, bound and gagged, appeared in the newspaper to a great outcry from the public, especially university students, Deb and I felt sickened and decided to go back to Champaign. The beef-and-corn-fed Midwest and its northern European settlers grew many very large people among the protesters and cops alike. Heavy winter clothing made them loom even larger. Deb and I were afraid of literally being trampled in further melees.

I didn't want to write about the trial after not being allowed to watch the proceedings, so I wrote a piece for *WIN* magazine describing the various ways I had witnessed people getting out of the Air Force using eccentric behavior or psychological appeals. They titled it "Creeps for Peace," which I was insulted by. How could an antiwar group call its allies "creeps?" Were they judging the shades of resistance legitimacy?

As the January 1970 spring semester started in Champaign, I discovered that the G.I. Bill would pay me double if I were married. In the middle of an antiwar demonstration on campus, when the state police blocked off all streets and about a hundred of us had to take shelter in a campus ministry building for the night, Deb and I stayed up, amped on adrenaline and ready to flee if the cops broke in. We felt a fear rising that Chicago and Champaign were more violent than the police state we'd left in Greece. The Unitarian minister who ran the place sat with us on a corner sofa, and we talked about Greece and torture and the police we'd eluded there.

As gray began spreading from the east, Deborah and I were holding hands as we talked with the minister.

"This is *déjà vu* for me," she told him. "I was caught in the Paris riots and got my knee sprained when the cops drove us into a cul-de-sac."

"How about you, Steve?" he asked.

"My mentor in Athens barely escaped torture by the security goons; he left immediately for Paris. I helped his wife and baby escape then had to escape myself."

"I watched blocks of Chicago burn in riots after King was killed," the pastor said. "We are really in a dark time."

After the day dawned and the state police withdrew their barricades, we had coffee with this empathetic antiwar Unitarian, and we decided to ask him if he would marry us. We didn't mention the G.I. Bill benefits.

He showed some concern. He quizzed us.

"Tell me why you want to take this step," he said.

We told him we loved each other, that we had been trusting each other's counsel and opinions and support for over two years now.

Deb said, "I've never been able to talk to anyone like I can with Steve. We've been near a lot of danger and craziness. We keep each other safe and sane." I was glad she didn't bring up the 10 percent schizophrenic diagnosis.

I said we had so many letters and conversations that made us love and trust each other. I was moved by having to put these feelings into words, and felt that everything we said was true, but I knew that neither of us was talking about the type of marriage our parents had. We were not going to refer to each other as wife and husband. Deb thought, like I did, that we didn't take any social institution seriously enough at that point to feel we were desecrating marriage, or deluding ourselves, or setting a trap for ourselves or even risking anything by getting married.

The pastor did the ceremony with just the two of us the next week. We went to the county courthouse to file the papers, and when the clerk asked Deb her last name, she said Brandybuck, one of the Tolkien hobbit characters. I kept a straight face and the old clerk didn't skip a beat. She'd heard every name and seen every type of person in her courthouse career. Apparently it wasn't for her to judge.

I wrote my mom that we had done it and she was upset that we hadn't come to Dallas to get married so she could be there. I told close friends that we were going to double our G.I. Bill money. Deb didn't tell her family. In total reaction to our many separations since we'd met three years before, and in some alchemy of the validation of loyalty and intimacy we'd declared to the minister, we were only apart one week over the next three years.

However, the Illinois winter of 1969 was long; snow first fell in October and stayed on the ground continuously until April. Six months of being cooped up inside and nine months of steady drug use later, Deb and I exploded at each other.

"No more psychedelics!" I yelled at her. "And we gotta cut down on weed!"

"Just because you can't handle it doesn't mean I have to cut down," she said.

"I can handle what I can handle, but you go away so far it's tearing us up!"

"I have learned how to play, Stephen. I go to a world of play on acid or mescaline or weed, and play is healing, and it's where art comes from. I think you're just afraid to let yourself go there, and you *need* to do that. If anything's tearing us up, it's your fears."

"Art? When we trip together, you wind up babbling the whole time and I don't see where it's led to any art at all! What have you produced? You don't share your trips, you're on broadcast mode the whole time! You don't need a partner, you need an audience! Deborah narrates the world, brought to you by Deborah! And now a word from Deborah!"

"So that's what it looks like to you? Too bad. I tell you about things I see when we're high because you don't seem capable of trusting your own eyes to see anything new. And whatever happens on trips doesn't just regurgitate as a piece of art to sell, ka-ching, ka-ching! It's way deeper than that."

So Deb and I began to slip and slide on personal ice as well as on the chaos around us. On May 4, 1970, four students were killed and nine others wounded by National Guard troops breaking up a mostly peaceful demonstration at Kent State University in Ohio.

At the record store, we had to have the breadth to deal with classical music buffs as well as rock and jazz people. We were often asked, "All this loud, pounding, wailing and shrieking music pouring out on records, these dope-scented concerts and 24/7 album-rock radio stations: what is this senseless noise?"

My young rock-fan coworkers and I retorted, "It isn't what Mr. and Mrs. America think: this loud music is the perfect mirror of the adult world's fear of out-of-control youth and blacks and the young and minorities' fears of out-of-control white power. It is whites' hysteric recoil from oncoming change, and youth's recoil from the officially sanctioned and funded firepower and brutality of local, state and federal police, with their license to repress, humiliate, punish, maim, kill or incarcerate the rebellious young, people of color and women who wanted a new America *really bad* — and we're going to the streets to get it."

So we responded, in so many words and/or variations.

Terror in Greece was followed, for us, by terror at home. So we hit the road for somewhere warmer than Illinois. We gave notice, sold excess stuff, and packed our essentials and favorites in a big trunk just like the ones I'd packed for Allan and Linda. It exactly fit into the rear space of our faded red VW bus. We rolled out of Champaign on a Saturday morning, cups of steaming coffee fogging the windshield.

Over the ensuing year we drove the country, blasting our radio and singing along with the Mamas and Papas, Grateful Dead, The Band, Jefferson Airplane, Marvin Gaye, and Sam and Dave. We were as much in search of ourselves as remaking connections with people. We stopped in Dallas to visit my mom (tense); in Santa Fe, where we felt a sweet echo of Greek villages in the soft contours of adobe; in San Francisco to hang out with my old Air Force friends from Mississippi (fun), to Oregon to visit Jack and Marlene from the ferry to Ios (weird); and to Vancouver, British Columbia, where we considered applying for resident status but were dissuaded by the Canadian border authorities wary of so many war resisters pouring across from the U.S. (sobering).

Wherever we went, we found we were not alone; we belonged to a whole generation of seekers, unmoored by recent national and international events. We crashed with friends, stayed in cheap motels, ate mostly at diners or picnicked at campgrounds. Even when we got the blues, the music of that youth migration soothed us. Carol King sang, "Doesn't anybody stay in one place anymore?" And James Taylor answered, "You can call out my name, and you know wherever I am, I'll come runnin', to see you again," and "Oh, I've seen fire and I've seen rain/I've seen lonely times when I could not find a friend … ." There was a shared soundtrack to our ups and downs that provided a bit of comfort in such a crazy time.

We wound up back in Austin (for me) in the summer of 1972, five years after I'd been drafted there. Deborah found her old San Antonio high school and Lady of the Lake College co-conspirator, Loretta Guerra, living in Austin. As high-school students, they had roamed San Antonio's downtown and Riverwalk cafés, smoking and grabbing unfinished wines and beers left on adjacent tables. It was on these escapades, Deb told me, that she was always taken for a Chicana by the local shoppers and cashiers, both brown and white. Loretta, born a Texas Chicana, was pretty and fair, with a languid suavité about her, and of course had the Guerra name. So on their adventures, Deborah often passed as Hispanic, too.

One morning at Loretta's and her boyfriend Jeff's, drinking strong coffee with a hearty breakfast of Loretta's pancakes, Jeff said, "Listen to what Tricky Dick's up to now." The lead story in that morning's newspaper was about Nixon's hard line on "war resisters and draft dodgers." Nixon announced that he was making the National Crime Information Center's computers available to the border patrol.

"What is he making available?" I asked.

"Says here 'The NCIC computer records center was launched January 27, 1967, in Washington, D.C., as the central FBI collection facility for criminal activity, like stolen cars and wanted fugitives.'"

"Wow!" I said. "They pushed the start button the very week I was drafted!"

"What synchronicity," Deborah said. "How creepy."

Jeff added, "Says the center houses a roomful of main-frame computers running large reels of tape as storage. The FBI has linked the NCIC computer to fifteen state and city computer systems, with Border Patrol the newest agency added to the list, so they could catch 'the war resisters and draft-dodgers who are eroding public support for the war in Vietnam.'"

"*Right!*" we cackled, dripping irony like syrup on our pancakes.

"It couldn't be the soaring deaths and dismemberments our boys are suffering!" Loretta said.

"Or the drug addiction of our draftees, or the napalm-bombing of peasant villages," Jeff added.

Jeff poured another round of coffee in our mugs and said, "You know Fort Hood? It's 60 miles north, the closest Army base to Austin? Its nickname is 'Fort Head,' for all the heroin and dope those guys bring home from Vietnam."

Mocking satire aside, Deb and I saw Nixon's computer help to the Border Patrol as a serious threat. Nixon's antagonistic comments about war resisters were widely circulated in the press, both underground and mainstream, although he had run for president in 1968 promising to end the war. Our experiences in Greece and in Chicago had been enough for Deb and I to fear Nixon's administration, but we got our proof when a trove of FBI documents released in the March 1972 issue of *WIN* magazine made public the existence of the FBI's notorious COINTELPRO operations.

COINTELPRO was J. Edgar Hoover's acronym for COunter-INTELligence PROgram, which he described to his FBI minions as designed "to expose, disrupt, misdirect, discredit, or otherwise neutralize" all movements that were critical of Hoover's definition of true Americanism. *WIN* was able to publish the secret FBI documents in March 1972, because a group calling itself the "Citizens Commission on the FBI" broke into a small FBI office in Media, Pennsylvania, a year before, in March 1971. The group was never identified or caught.

The underground press was all over the revelations about COINTELPRO, which told the wider society what activists had known all along in the 1960s: that the FBI had infiltrated all the antiwar groups, civil-rights groups, labor organizations, church groups, women's rights groups, and American Indian and Chicano groups — not only spying on them but also planting provocateurs who spread false rumors among activists and pushed for more violence in the groups' pursuit of their goals. COINTELPRO helped all branches of law enforcement kill, jail or drive into exile most of the leaders of AIM (the American Indian Movement), the Weather Underground, Students for a Democratic Society, the Student Non-Violent Coordinating Committee, and the Black Panther Party. Although Hoover claimed he had disbanded COINTELPRO as a response to the public furor when his secret sabotage operation was made public, it had been the perfect counterrevolutionary army to disrupt citizen movements for justice and government accountability for over ten years.

Deborah and I decided we'd had enough of being back in what we now called "the U.S.S.A.," satirizing Paul McCartney's song "Back in the U.S.S.R.," the opening cut on their double *White Album* in 1968. Paul's song was an homage to Chuck Berry's "Back in the U.S.A." Both songs were upbeat can't-stand-still tributes that we loved and sang along with, but the reality we were much more conscious of was the dark view Dylan expressed in "Desolation Row." We wanted to return to village life and rural landscapes, and Mexico was only 220 miles from Austin. Mexico became our new Greece. But we feared Nixon's net would trap us when we came back into the United States.

We had just read an anthropology book on the Huichol, the western Mexico tribe that maintains a peyote pilgrimage at the heart of their religion. The ceremonial use of a hallucinogen was the sort of news that caught the ear of many countercultural folks at the time. But for Deborah, the Huichol were apparently more: they embodied remoteness, mystery and small stature along with their practice of "dreaming" to "see their lives" with the help of the mescaline in peyote.

Their leader at the time, according to the book, was a shaman named Ramon Medina Silva. Deb said, Aha! She'd found a family name for her new identity; now she just needed a new first name. She soon chose the first name Maguey (pronounced muh-GAY). These blue-green agaves grew to huge sizes around Austin, up to six feet high and ten feet across, and we saw that magueys are a Mexican landscape icon as we perused the book by our new favorite photographer, Mexico's Manuel Alvarez Bravo.

Mexico became the perfect stage for Deborah's morphing into Maguey Medina Silva. Within a year, her alter ego took on a life of its own that completely closed the door on her former life and took our relationship to its fateful conclusion. It didn't feel that way at the time. We were having a blast learning to live on the streets of Mexico, discovering its tasty food, its warm people, its deep history and dramatic landscapes. But looking back, I see the scenes popping into sharp focus in which Deborah added layers of Maguey's new identity.

Mexico was just the escape we'd hoped it would be from U.S. war, riots and consumerism. Like so many adventurers before us who had faced new people with a smile and broken Spanish, we felt surrounded by friends everywhere we went. We knew we were part of a long line of kindred souls, because several people called us *existentialistas* and always wanted to talk. We traveled by bus, having sold our VW bus before we left Austin.

The key experience for both of us was a five month stay in Pátzcuaro, a National Heritage town half an hour west of Morelia by bus. The Indian market town drew tourists and collectors of native art. Deb and I were carrying our cameras that I had bought with my Air Force separation money. They were Olympus Pen-F single-lens reflexes, the miniature marvels of the late sixties. We roamed Pátzcuaro and the pueblos around the town, staying for pennies a day at the scroungy Hotel Pito Perez and developing our film in our room.

The center of cultural life in Pátzcuaro, for tourists and local tribal people alike, was a museum of the popular arts that was full of Tarascan Indian masks, carvings, textiles, pottery and copper goods. It was presided over by an imperious middle-aged Mexicana named Teresa Davalos de Luft. Doña Teresa adopted us as star guests and students, and held forth on local arts and culture and the Spanish language. She took Deborah under her wing, while her German husband, Enrique Luft, asked me to photograph his surrealist paintings and took me to bars, where he identified me as "mi nieto," my nephew. Enrique was a good-hearted alcoholic and Teresa, a forceful and dedicated teacher. From them I learned my limits of mescal, tequila and *cerveza,* while Deb learned more and more Indian lore and Spanish vocabulary.

From Pátzcuaro, we made a fantastic loop by buses from Guadalajara to Puerto Vallarta, down the Pacific Coast to Puerto Escondido on the far south shore of Oaxaca state then over to Oaxaca city and up to Mexico City. This two-month road trip was even richer than Greece had been, because we got to stare spellbound at the public murals by "Los Tres Grandes" — José Clemente Orozco, David Alfaro

Siqueiros and Diego Rivera — and converse with beautiful native people wearing clothes that were works of art and selling stunning beadwork, pottery and woven designs bright with color and detail. We finished this tour off by calling the photographer Manuel Alvarez Bravo — his number was in the phone book and we called from a pay phone — who invited us to his home for coffee, hors d'oeuvres and a visit.

Back in Pátzcuaro, we faced crises: our plan to make some money by teaching English fell through, because, as Señora Davalos told us, the local police were not tolerating Americans teaching English unless they had a permit issued by a Mexican school. We were running out of money. I had left a thousand dollars of my Air Force lump sum in an Austin bank to tide us over when we returned to the States, but buying our VW van, our camera gear and sleeping bags, buying film and developing chemicals, printing paper, gasoline and food over the two years of traveling had nearly depleted our $7,000 fund. The *coup de grace* was that I got a terrible dysentery bug after nine months of eating from street vendors and local restaurants with no gastrointestinal troubles. We had concluded that we were charmed and laughed at the Americanos who complained about "Montezuma's Revenge." But I didn't treat it soon enough. After three days I was too weak to walk. Deb found a doctor, who took one look at me and growled, "You stupid Americans! One more day and he'd be dead!" It took three days on an I.V. drip and penicillin to rehydrate me and kill the bugs, but I had amazing color dreams of Alvarez Bravo's photographs (in the books we had, they were all black and white), plus my own hallucinations. It was a close call. It humbled me.

I was released from the clinic and we were on the road again on a train going north to Juarez. We were almost broke when we rolled through the wide northern deserts and back into the U.S. at El Paso.

We were detained for an hour by the Border Patrol.

"What is your citizenship?" the border patrol officer demanded.

"American," I answered, looking him in the eye. "Born August 18, 1944, in Washington, D.C."

He seemed convinced by my accent.

"And why are you traveling with ... Miss Maguey Medina Silva?"

"We're married," I said. "We're writers and photographers."

Deb produced a Mexican document verifying that we were married in El Paso two years earlier. The border patrol officer conferred with someone in the next room and let us sit for another half hour while he hassled others.

"I'm admitting you two," he said when he returned, "but Miss Medina Silva only on a six-month educational visa. You'll have to reapply at the end of six months for an American marriage license and present passports at that time." We could have avoided that small irritation by carrying our American marriage license, but alas, it had two names on it that we weren't using in Mexico, so it would have complicated things significantly.

I was still weak from the dysentery. We hailed a taxi with a rush of relief and had him take us to the I-10 highway that headed north. It wasn't Nixon's enemies list that almost kept us from reentering our country; it was Deborah in her red rebozo with her strange patois of accents. I was admiring, amused and grateful for the connections her chameleonic skills had brought to our nine months in Mexico. And I believed that the performance phase was over, now that we were crossing the line back to the USA.

# NINETEEN

The late summer sky was clear, with a few high clouds; the air was warm and the breeze light as we hitchhiked north from El Paso on I-10. After 30 miles it meets I-25 at Las Cruces, New Mexico. One ride took us to Las Cruces. The jagged peaks of the Organ Mountains on our right overlooked Cruces like a spectacular dinosaur pushing its spine up through the desert floor. From there we got a ride from a university professor all the way to Albuquerque. We were in post-adventure relaxation, comfortable watching the New Mexico basins and ranges roll by, so much like northern Mexico. Our ride let us out on Albuquerque's north side, where a black man in a suit driving a Cadillac picked us up and took us to Santa Fe. He kindly drove us all the way downtown to drop us off. The dusk had deepened, and our sleepy eyes snapped open to a milling throng filling the old town square.

"What's going on?" I asked of some young revelers passing by as we stood on the west side of the plaza, backpacks on our backs and confusion on our faces.

"Fiestas, man!" a guy said. "They just burned Zozobra!"

"Burned what?"

"Old Man Gloom, man. Don't you know?"

"No, we just got to town."

"Great timing, man, it's the biggest night of the year in Santa Fe. There's like 20,000 people here for Zozobra."

"Where can we find a phone?" I asked.

The four young people grinning at us all pointed diagonally across the plaza to a three-story pueblo-like building.

"They have pay phones at La Fonda hotel," the guy said as they rejoined the river of people surging along the wide sidewalk.

We dug into our wallets to find the names and phone numbers of the two friends of friends we hoped would put us up for a night or two until we got our bearings. The La Fonda was jammed with young people loudly drinking at the two bars inside and stylishly dressed older couples going into the high-end restaurant in the courtyard. We got change for a dollar from a waiter and tried our numbers. Holding one forefinger into my right ear against the noise, I heard through the earpiece the complete opposite: cautious voices coming from quiet homes.

"Wow, didn't you know tonight is the start of Fiestas?" asked one.

"Steve who?" said the other. "Whose friend? Oh. Well, we've got a full house. The town's jammed. Sorry."

I asked both households in turn if we could just unroll our sleeping bags in their backyards until morning. "Uh … no, that won't be possible," both said.

I looked at Deb; we watched hope drain from each other's faces.

"Let's see if there's a hostel," Deb said. We shouldered our packs and went out into the plaza sidewalk crowds again. Nobody we asked knew of a hostel. Most laughed at the mere thought of our finding a bed on this night. As we looked up and down the street in front of La Fonda, a green 1950s' Chevy pickup pulled over to the curb.

"You guys need a ride?" said a handsome Chicano guy at the wheel, with high cheekbones and light-colored eyes.

"We need a place to stay," I said.

"Hop in," he said, "I know a place."

We threw our packs in the bed and I let Deb in first. Her short legs rested on the transmission hump.

"I'm Beto," he said.

"I'm Maguey," she said.

*Oh*, I thought, *she's back.* I reached over her to shake hands with Beto.

"I'm Steve. We just got in town from nine months in Mexico." Beto's eyes lit up. He looked us over. In the oncoming headlights I saw his eyes were green and his smile toothy.

"So where is this place?" I asked.

He said his family had some land on the edge of town. Because of Zozobra, their house was full, but there was a dirt road leading off their land that had a little campsite.


We sat holding our knees around our campfire of piñon and juniper sticks as the stars wheeled across the sky. We were at about 7,500 feet and the night was growing cold. Beto went down to his family's house and brought back an armload of blankets and a plastic jug of water. Another trip and he brought back a dish of barbecued brisket covered in foil. We ate and got drowsy. He had what was left of a joint and we had a toke or two apiece. He said their house was so full that he preferred camping out here with us. With Orion high in the sky we spread the blankets and unrolled our bags in the bed of the pickup and put one heavy blanket over all of us. It never occurred to me to put myself between Deb and Beto. She was in the middle again.

I woke before dawn and slipped out of the pickup bed to relieve my bladder a ways up the road. I looked over the city lights and stars and reviewed our journey so far. We were back in the U.S. after such a long stream of adventures. I was tired of the road and wanted us to live here.

When I got back to the truck, Deborah's and my relationship was over. The blanket was moving up and down.

It flashed through my mind that if it had been rape, she would have yelled, and in the quiet night I couldn't have missed a sound. I was only 20 yards from the truck. Numb, I walked straight away toward a nearby arroyo that had a small stream of water running in it. *I should have ripped the blanket off and confronted them.* But I was so overcome with sadness and betrayal I just waited for her to come to me.

She appeared beside me in the gray light. We didn't look at each other.

"So was it good for you?" I asked hollowly. "How could you do this?"

"It was okay," she mumbled. "I'm sorry."

"Did he force you?"

"No."

Apart from my sadness at what she'd done, I was seething at the predatory Beto.

"You tell that piece of shit he's going to take me into town right now. I don't know where we are out here and I don't care what you do or where you go. We're done."

I rolled my sleeping bag up and kicked hers and the blankets to the far end of the truck bed. I rode in the back and got out at the plaza, giving them the finger as they drove away. I walked toward La Fonda and had to stop and puke at the curb. The sun wasn't up over the mountains yet, but the sky was getting bright. No cars rolled by on the plaza, and only a few early walkers were out. The streets were littered with paper and plastic cups from the reveling crowds the night before. A guy walking by asked me if I was all right. I said yes but I could use a handkerchief. He handed me a blob of paper napkins he had in his back pocket and I wiped my mouth. I asked him if there was a church nearby. He said yes, well, that's the cathedral right there, of course.

"I don't want a Catholic church."

"OK, well, there's a Presbyterian one about five blocks that way. It's adobe-looking, where the streets fork."

I was suddenly sure that somebody at a church would understand that I needed some help. I didn't want to start spending what little money I had left on motel rooms, and I didn't want to talk to anybody I knew, much less to my family. I wanted to start over right here, near this plaza that was so much like Mexico, breathing this high-desert air. As I walked toward the adobe Presbyterian church I breathed deeply in and deeply out. *Steady, boy.*

# TWENTY

The assistant pastor at the church was wearing Birkenstocks with athletic socks, jeans and a suede jacket over a Moody Blues T-shirt. He was sweeping the litter off the sidewalk beside the church entrance when I came up. He got me some coffee from the vestry kitchen and sat down to listen to me. He said they had a homeless lunch that day and every Saturday that I was welcome to. He got me some donuts from the kitchen, and I told him my abbreviated story.

"So you're a Vietnam vet? And a college guy?"

"I never went to Vietnam, just to Greece. And yeah, I was in grad school in English when they drafted me." He was interested in talking about Greece and my experiences in Mexico, but I told him what I really needed was a room to sleep in for a night or two and I didn't have enough money for a motel.

"If you'd help me sweep around the church and set up the tables for the free lunch today, I'll pay you a few bucks. We have a garage apartment behind our house, my wife and me. It's on the east side, off Garcia Street. You can stay there for a couple of nights."

Another angel. I ate with the homeless guys and went home with the assistant pastor that afternoon. His name was Marty. He had a husky voice and some gray at the temples.

"I see your camera there," he said.

"Yeah, we were taking pics all over Mexico."

"I know a couple of photographers. They might be of some help to you."

One of them managed a compound of funky adobe apartments and tiny houses off Sandoval Street, about six blocks from the church. His name was Michael Tincher, and we became friends. In two days I had a key to a vacant apartment attached to his that needed repair before it could be rented. Michael and I agreed that I could stay there for free if I would repair the wooden floor that was cracking apart from years of leaks and muddy boot traffic. He said I'd have to keep drapes over the floor-to-ceiling windows set deeply into the adobe walls so the owner wouldn't suspect I was living there rent-free on her regular visits to collect rents from Tincher.

It was called the José Street Compound. With older pickups, a fading VW bus, and my neighbor's flatbed truck carving and recarving the ruts through the open space in the middle, and piles of chopped firewood near most of the houses, it was a northern New Mexico village surviving just out of sight of gentrifying Santa Fe. I had coffee with Tinch at his studio/house every morning and found the Jefferson Street Soup Company for lunch, a rustic café run by two women a few blocks south on Sandoval. It became my hangout and office. I had a neighborhood. I had a world.

For a month I renailed and patched my wood floor, covering knothole gaps with pieces of an old license plate — hammered flat, trimmed to size — and nailed every inch around its edges. The mice and the rats below had to move to a different house to raise their pink babies. I replumbed the ancient claw-foot tub. I had to dig up the blocked drainpipe and find where it connected to the compound sewer line. It's always good to know where a town's sewer system is and what sort of crap — literal or political — is flowing through it beneath the human dramas and hijinks being staged above, as I had learned in Athens.

After sanding and three coats of brown floor paint, I had a new floor, made a desk and a work table, and on this level and private platform I began rebuilding my life. On a wood run to Rowe Mesa I met a guy who said the state legislature hired proofreaders. A new session would begin in January and I should check it out. This necessitated a haircut and some new clothes, paid for by extra wages from Tinch for repairing walls, windows and doors on other units around the compound.

I applied for the proofreader job at the state capitol, a three-story-tall circular building known as The Merry Roundhouse in the press. I aced the test and began the 60-day session as the only guy in a group of four women. We sat in pairs reading aloud to each other. One would read the newly proposed revisions of state law that had been typed into bills from the legislative process, enunciating every comma, period, parenthesis and semicolon, as the other traced the wording in the old version, published in bound volumes.

I had returned to my roots, analyzing language and reading aloud legal prose in a state capital, much like reading the legislative news over the air at LBJ's station in Austin. This state capital was also full of young people experiencing its unique Mexican flavor, as adventurous young people had been since the art colony's heydays in the 1920s and '30s. Now Santa Fe's ski area drew middle-class athletes; St. John's College drew students of the classics from across the country; and the New Age drew bohemians and the alternative-therapy crowd. The three massage schools in particular filled the downtown area with beaded, macraméd women wearing sandals and handwoven shawls. Devoted to hands-on bodywork, their closets were full of clothes in green and purple; they outnumbered the young men two to one; and the dance floors were jammed with sinuous dancing to the music of Eliza Gilkyson, who lived in Santa at the time. The result was that I had plenty of girlfriends and didn't miss Deborah.

One day in the spring of 1974 I came home to the José Street compound to find Deborah sitting on my porch. She had found me by asking around at the Soup Company. My anger and hurt had faded into curiosity at how she was doing as Maguey. We hugged softly like old pals, and over tea in my living room she announced why she'd come: she had been hanging out at the Institute of American Indian Arts — at the time, right on Cerrillos Road south of downtown. She had met some Indian filmmakers there who told her she should apply at a school called the Anthropology Film Center.

"They're training native people to be the first Indians to shoot and produce their own films," she said. "It's way up Canyon Road, beyond the galleries, in Santa Fe Canyon. I came to ask you for a ride up there, and to ask you to apply too, because we both have our pictures from Mexico. I bet they'd like our shots from the Museo in Pátzcuaro and the natives we met there. Maybe you could get the G.I. Bill money again."

Carroll Williams, the former Hollywood sound man on the James Bond film *Thunderball* who founded the center, did like our pictures and admitted us to the center's next class. Carroll's wife was Joan Swayze, a Ph.D. anthropologist and the daughter of John Cameron Swayze, a television news anchor from the fifties, the first to be called an "anchor." Deborah, as Maguey, became friends with the Indian guys who were the center's first native grads. Their group was called Circle Films. Not wanting to be in the same three-month class as Deborah, I waited for the next one, through which I met local filmmakers and dubbed the voice-over narration for a short film. El Gringo was riding again.

Over the next year, Deb met me for coffee every couple of months or so to tell me about her visits to the Chicano free school, Tonantzín, out on Agua Fría road, where she traded quips with the painter and activist Sammie Leyba, whose murals of Chicanismo had blossomed on a dozen buildings in the city. She had also followed Circle Films members Larry Little Bird, of the Laguna and Santo Domingo pueblos, and George Burdeau, of the Blackfeet tribe, out to California and Spokane to help make their films.

The last time I saw her in Santa Fe, she popped in for a visit from the West Coast looking sad and evasive. She wanted to build a sweat lodge and hold a ceremony to heal her frazzled spirit. The ground was frozen and we couldn't dig a fire pit, so the woman I was living with let us rig up a tarp around a wood stove, which we filled with big smooth rocks and fired up. As we sat in the hot steam rich with sage and mint under the tarp, Deborah finally put an honest question to me that had lingered in the air whenever I'd thought of her over the last two years.

She said, in a small girlish voice: "What's wrong with me?"

I knew the sweat lodge demanded honesty and compassion. I thought for a minute about how to answer her in a true way but a compassionate way.

Finally I said, "You're trying to be somebody you're not. That must be incredibly hard. Anyway it's not working well." Tears rolled down her face as she shook a rattle and tried to hum some native chant she'd learned.

"Thank you," she said. "You're my brother."

Was Deborah a con, a compulsive liar, a talented impressionist, a wounded seeker, a multiple personality, or some combination of all those? Was she emotionally and mentally affected by some chemical imbalance in her brain? I'll never know.

I met one of those Santa Fe massage therapists who had a sense of humor and a great quick mind. She also had three boys — four, six and eight — and was six months removed from an abusive marriage. I married her, and we moved to Albuquerque in 1978, where the boys could get better schooling and I could return to graduate school at the University of New Mexico. I set out to apply to the English department, picking up the thread that had been snapped by my being drafted. But on my way there with my application, a final angel reappeared. He was Steve Choisser, who had worked alongside me at the Champaign Discount Records store. I remembered that he was a writer, too. We stared at each other in delight and disbelief, then stood in the hall catching up. After all I'd done and the miles I'd covered, the odds of Choisser and I being in the same English department office at the same transitory moment, 1,200 miles and almost four years from when we'd last been together, seemed the most improbable of all my encounters. I told him my plan to return to English studies.

"From what I remember about you and your writing," he said, "the American Studies department would be a much better fit for you. It's one floor up. I can show you."

Steve said he was just leaving for California, and I wished him well. Then I talked with the chair of American Studies. It did fit me, to a T. There were courses in culture, politics, history, ethnic studies and the American West. I could choose classes and professors from other departments and set my own course of study. Choisser was right: this was a program in which I could put all of my experiences of the last five years into context, with the country and the many different voices calling for change. I submitted my application, put in a request for a teaching assistantship, and left the Humanities building, crossing the wide brick campus plaza toward the tall adobe-style library.

I crossed the paths of students walking across the plaza on errands in every direction. Many of them had black hair and bronze skin, and I heard words in Spanish as I walked. I laughed out loud as I replayed the chance meeting with Choisser and how it led me into American Studies. I was back in the USA and back to studying the world I lived in. I had yearned for experience, and it had come to me from all directions. I had longed for guides, and they consistently popped up in front of me. I had faced war, segregation, fascism, and torture. I had missed out on graduate school at my first try; but on my wartime odyssey, I had become friends with scholars, war resisters, artists, mental patients, elites and street people, Greeks and Mexicans. I felt a surge of excitement as I joined these New Mexico University people in this public square, busily working toward their futures and the country's.

# EPILOGUE

The urge to write this book started in 2005, when I began ransacking my memory about my odyssey as a young man. My birth name, and my name through the events chronicled in this book, was Stephen Larner. Repeated mention of torture in the media, beginning in 2004 with the revelations of prisoner abuse at the Abu Ghraib prison in Iraq, reminded me of my brush with it in Athens 36 years earlier.

Thanks to Internet search engines, I located Allan Wenger and Jim Cuomo for the first time in all those years. They were living a mile apart in Paris, unaware of each other. In January 2006, I went to see them, this time as an adjunct professor. I had been teaching American Studies, Sociology and General Honors for over 20 years, including a two-year stint as a Fulbright lecturer in Germany — Frankfurt for a year and another year in Hamburg — as Germany struggled to reunite its East and West halves. I was seasoned as a researcher and as a teacher of multicultural courses and students, and I needed to reunite with these two old friends, Allan and Jim, who had been key actors in my journey as a younger man.

Allan and his wife, Linda, had become teachers of English at Paris schools, Allan rising to headmaster. Jim had brought his band Spoils of War to Paris in 1970 and continued living there on his own until 2012 as a composer and leader of small jazz groups playing in bars. The Paris conservatory invited him to conduct its student orchestra in a retrospective celebration of his compositions in 2008. He is now living in Australia, active with the Moreland City Band.

The last time I saw Deborah was in 1980, when she came to my door in Albuquerque with a baby daughter in her arms. The baby was clean and chubby, with dark skin and black hair. The baby's father, a guy named Beto with long black hair down his back, waited in the car. She looked neat and wore brown jeans, desert boots and a huipil top. I held the baby and looked into her tiny face and wondered: what will life bring her? I hoped the little girl might exert some gravitational pull of stability on her small wandering mother.

I had then, and have now, great compassion for Deb. Hers was an expression—extreme and daring, to be sure—of an impulse that is woven into the American fabric: she wanted to escape her personal history and start over as somebody new. As this book was going to press, I found the letters she wrote me from the outposts of her travels after we broke up. Also bound with them in an old leather binder were all of the Spanish vocabulary studies we began in Austin and she continued in California. There were some journal entries and fiction stories she wrote. She was a serious and hardworking student in all of the creative paths she took.

The last I heard of her, she was reported as found dead from a faulty gas heater that winter of 1980 in Nevada City, California, in bed with her child. But the person who called me with that news denied it when I found her years later, saying "but it was you who called me." I visited Nevada City in 2010 and searched town and county records but found no trace of her. It could have been a suicide, a murder, or a story to cover another identity change. I may never know. It was an enigma wrapped in a mysterious burrito, to Hispanicize Churchill.

In 2009, I returned to Greece for the first time since I'd fled the Colonels, this time with the love of my life, my third wife, Donna LeFurgey. After the flawed marriage with Deborah and the end of the marriage to the mother of the three boys I helped raise for fifteen years, I met Donna, an architectural designer, at the Adobe Bar in Taos in 1998.

Greece had been struggling back toward democracy since the Colonels were overthrown in 1974. I found Athiná, working as a special aide to the minister of culture. In a lovely irony, her office was in the once-infamous Bouboulinas Street building across from the National Museum of Archaeology from which Allan escaped and where Yannis endured torture. After the Colonels, Athiná earned advanced degrees from the Sorbonne in Paris and Princeton in the U.S., but now that I was back to see her in 2009, both of us, of course, looking very different, she barely remembered me.

She hadn't used her English in years. But I was thrilled to hear that she had avoided the Colonels, continued her education, as I had, and that the blood she coughed when I last saw her had been from severe bronchitis, not tuberculosis. Athiná took me and Donna to her favorite restaurant, called Alexandria, owned by her good friend, named Cleopatra. We only had one evening to talk, and language was again a problem. My photos from that return to Greece are posted on my website, www.stevefoxtaos.com.

The old Athens International Airport, including the U.S. Athenai Air Base, was torn down in 1980, as was the Iraklion Air Base on Crete. The Prime Minister of Greece in 2011 was George Papandreou, the son of Andreas Papandreou, whose probable election as prime minister in 1967 led to the Colonels' coup.

Since the 2008 global economic downturn and the European Union's financial-austerity policies, it has saddened me to see Greece struggling with massive unemployment, the collapse of its economy and its inability to properly protect its rich archaeological heritage. Greece is now the prime doorway to Europe for illegal immigrants seeking a way into the European Union's prosperity, political liberalism and social welfare. Their numbers have overwhelmed Greece and stoked the flames of xenophobia, contributing to the resurgence of the Greek far right, as it has in all European countries.

I feel blessed to have lived the life I have, including being drafted. I am still opposed to war and the militarization of our police and the expansion of mass collection of data by the National Security Agency, now appropriately called the "Hoovering up" of data. Like many my age, now near 70, I wonder if we'll ever again have the dedicated and courageous mass resistance to racism, environmental destruction, misogyny and war that we had in the 1960s and 1970s. My role continues to be to write and teach at the college level about what has happened to our country, especially in the last fifty years, from a people's-history point of view, like that pioneered by Howard Zinn, Martin Luther King Jr., Rebecca Solnit, Bill Moyers, Taos's John Nichols, and many others.

Another gratifying revelation came as this book went to press in early 2014: five of the eight humble and patriotic whistle-blowers, from Haverford College in Philadelphia, who broke into the FBI office in Media, Pennsylvania, back in 1971 identified themselves and took credit for their uncovering of the COINTEL program, as detailed in Betty Medsger's book *The Burglary* (Random House, January 2014.) The struggles will go on, and we can all have a part in them — one day, one person, one challenge, one angel at a time.

# ACKNOWLEDGMENTS

This book would have been vastly poorer without long talks and bottles of wine with Allan Wenger, my mentor in Athens in 1968–69 and my memory guide again in Paris in 2006 and 2009. The personal archives and memories of Jim Cuomo, Jeff Woodruff, Athiná Skina, Becky Sakellariou, and Andy Dennison clarified many details for me.

I am so grateful to "the B Girls": Becky Lenzini for moving to Taos and founding Nighthawk Press; the terrific Barb Scott for her meticulous design of the book; and fellow Taos memoirist Bonnie Lee Black for her deep insight into what to leave in, what to leave out. Thanks also to Kathleen Munroe for her design of the covers and selection of the title font.

Angels with sharpies who read earlier drafts include Dawn Marano, Gregory Martin, Dan Mueller, Sean Murphy, and Mark Sundeen. Without the 15-year run of the Taos Summer Writers Conference, founded and still directed by Dr. Sharon Oard Warner, founder of the University of New Mexico Creative Writing Program, I might not have met Greg, Dan and Mark.

My deepest thanks go to my wife, Donna LeFurgey, who expertly fielded (or avoided) my obsessions, moods, absences both physical and virtual, and the amounts of money I spent on this book over the seven years I tangoed with it.

# ABOUT THE AUTHOR

Steve Fox lives in Taos, New Mexico, with his wife, two Aussie shepherd dogs and four chickens. His parents' ancestors included writers and editors going back to the early 1800s. Fox has taught writing and American Studies at the University of New Mexico in Albuquerque, as a Fulbrighter at the universities of Frankfurt and Hamburg in Germany, and now at UNM-Taos. He is the author of *Toxic Work—Women Workers at GTE-Lenkurt* (1991) and an editor and journalist. He has had shows of his photography in Albuquerque and Taos. Visit him at stevefoxtaos.com.

## Interior Photographs

Page 5. Linda and Allan, temple to Hephaestus, Agora, Athens. c. 1966. Courtesy Allan Wenger.

Page 24. Deborah Cuomo, age 21. 1969. By Steve Fox.

Page 43. Jacqueline Kennedy, Lucia and David Cuomo. 1963. AP Wire Photo.

Page 45. Dominic Cuomo promoted to Sr. Master Sgt., c. 1964. Air Force photo, courtesy Jim Cuomo.

Page 50. Theseus and the Amazon queen Antiope, displayed where found in Athens subway excavation. By Steve Fox.

Page 79. Shepherd driving flock on highway, Peloponnese, 2009. By Steve Fox.

Page 85. Temple to Apollo, Delphi, 2009. By Steve Fox

Page 104. Allan and Linda on stage, Athens, c. 1967. Courtesy Allan Wenger.

Page 109. Steve Larner (Fox) gets 8-ball award from Col. Bert Fisher, 1969. Air Force photo.

Page 129. Allan in Greek cap, c. 1966. Courtesy Linda Carter.

Page 171. Typical old island village passageway, Hora on Patmos, 2009. By Steve Fox.

Page 231. Athiná Skina, Donna LeFurgey, Steve Fox, Restaurant Alexandria, Athens, 2009. Courtesy Cleopatra.

Made in the USA
San Bernardino, CA
27 April 2014